T0380766

MANKIND; GOD'S MOST AWESOME CREATION

(The TRUE Origin of Man)

Lindsey K. Ham Sr.

God created this universe and all life in it (Genesis 1, 1-28 KJV). There was no spontaneous big bang and the universe does NOT exist because of a spontaneous, evolutionary, purposeless process. What are human beings? Where are we? How do different variables in this physical realm work together? These, and a lot more questions are answered in this book, and may God bless you to understand The Truth about everything after reading it.

Print information available on the last page

Rev. date: 02/12/2019

To order additional copies of this book, contact:
Xlibris
1-888-795-4274
www.Xlibris.com
Orders@Xlibris.com

MANKIND; GOD'S MOST AWESOME CREATION

(THE TRUE ORIGIN OF MAN)

Mr. Lindsey K. Ham Sr.

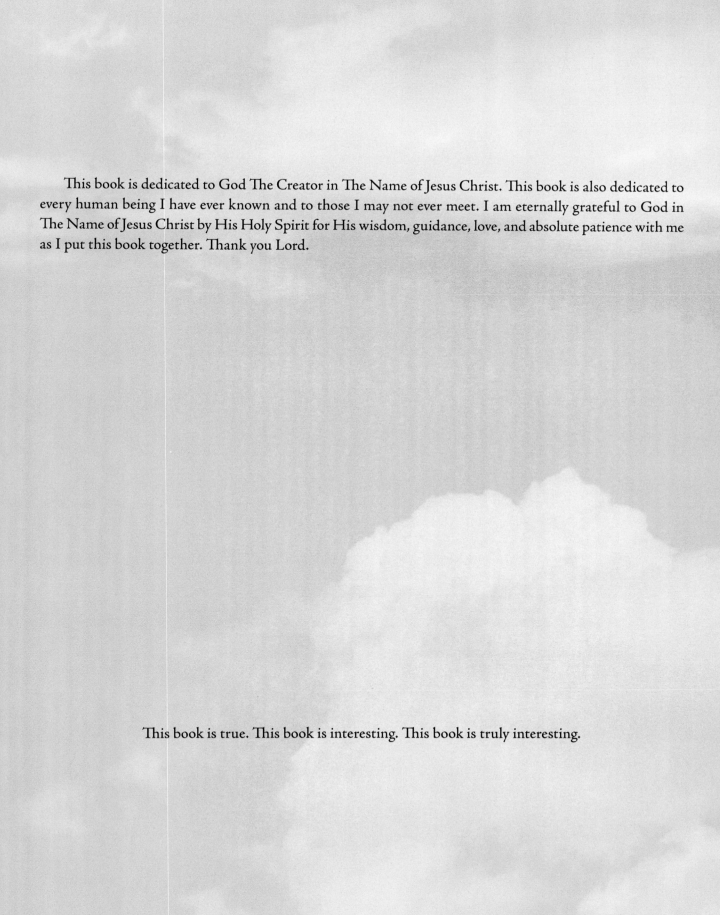

This book is dedicated to God The Creator in The Name of Jesus Christ. This book is also dedicated to every human being I have ever known and to those I may not ever meet. I am eternally grateful to God in The Name of Jesus Christ by His Holy Spirit for His wisdom, guidance, love, and absolute patience with me as I put this book together. Thank you Lord.

This book is true. This book is interesting. This book is truly interesting.

PREFACE

The universe and organic beings are not just spontaneous things that happened; God created everything. Spontaneity means that things happen at random for no reason at all, and there is factually/scientifically no such thing as anything being "spontaneous". The very meaning of "spontaneous" is **"without purpose"** and we ALL KNOW that there are *many purposes* for each and every thing in existence both good and evil, spiritual and physical. If human beings are only "spontaneous things" which happen to exist, then it would be impossible for human beings to ask the question, "Why am I here?". Atheists, unsaved people, "religious" folks, and also people who believe in the Truth of Jesus Christ, all ask that question and of course …..we all do. God purposefully created each and every one of us, so we are naturally infused with the inquest, "Why am I here?". We are definitely aware of the existence of "purpose" because "Why?" is an inquisition *about* purpose initiated by our subconscious/spiritual knowledge that there are many reasons for each and every thing.

An "atheist" is a person who has decided they will not believe God exists in spite of the multiplicity of obvious realities. Thousands of people from ALL of the modern scientific disciplines worldwide (many of whom are self-proclaimed atheists) are being used by Satan (the devil; humanity's sworn spiritual enemy who has already been sentenced by God Almighty to eternal damnation) to intentionally confuse scientific information about physical facts. Scientific studies from each and every discipline CLEARLY show that God created everything.

What is The Truth? The Truth is The Almighty, Omnipotent, Omnipresent, Creator of everything; God, In The Name of Jesus Christ, by His Holy Spirit. This means that God Is All-powerful, He is everywhere at the same time, and that God has always been and He will always be… God is. Modern scientists often use terms like "intelligent design" as a roundabout way to acknowledge that God created everything without openly humbling themselves to the Living Creator…..but **every** knee SHALL bow and **every** tongue SHALL confess Almighty God in the end (Romans 14:11; Isaiah 45:23 KJV).

MANKIND; GOD'S MOST AWESOME CREATION
(The True Origin of Man)

CONTENTS

CREATION

FROM THE BIBLE; GENESIS: CHAPTER (1)

Verse 1: God created Space and the Earth.

Verse 3: God created the Sun.

Verses 4 and 5: God spun the earth around to start the revolutions required to make nights and days.

Verses 6 and 7: God created the sky (the atmosphere).

Verse 9: God formed and separated the oceans, seas, and the dry lands.

Verse 10: God named the Earth.

Verse 11: God created the plants, flowers, trees, etc.

Verses 14, 15, and 16: God created the moon and the stars.

Verses 20 thru 25: God *spiritually* created each animal (there was no evolution).

Verses 26 thru 31: God *spiritually* created mankind; male AND female.

FROM THE BIBLE; GENESIS: CHAPTER (2)

Verse 7: NOW God made man's ***physical body*** from the ground and breathed the already created male AND female *spirit of man* into that one body.

Verses 18 thru 20: NOW God physically made the already spiritually created animals (this is why each species is limited to only physically expressing its' unique spiritual characteristics). Adam (the man AND woman) then named each animal.

Verses 21 thru 25: God put Adam (each half of the spirit of man) to sleep and then physically separated the woman from the man. The spirits of both sexes were created BEFORE God made different physical bodies to contain men and women.

CHAPTER ONE

HUMAN CONSCIOUSNESS: ATTENTIONAL AWARENESS

I can watch someone from across a room while listening to another conversation between two different people going on behind me, while at the same time thinking about stopping and buying some eggs from that little yellow store on my way home so I can see that pretty girl who works there again. Human beings are complex and we spiritually plan things while still being attentive to inputs from our different physical senses as we direct them according to our personal will. We also sometimes intensify our physical senses by concentrating them on selected areas of interests, and some of these physical indicators of sensory intensifications are squinting to see better, closing our eyes to hear better, or making particular facial expressions so we can concentrate more. *The ability to pay attention* is therefore a manifestation of physical consciousness and we each remember all kinds of information we have paid attention to while we've been conscious during our lifetimes. ALL OF US KNOW for instance, that spontaneous materialization of anything does not happen. Spontaneous materialization (if there was such a thing) would be the sudden appearance of random matter on its own *from nothing and for no reason*. For instance, a group of people are sitting on a beach when suddenly a pecan pie with a baseball on it, inside of a used tire slides down a wall which also suddenly appeared out of nowhere. Spontaneous things do not happen and we all know that. While I'm riding a bicycle, 14 purple vacuum cleaners and a Musk Ox having a baby are not going to spontaneously appear out of nowhere on a pancake on the sidewalk in front of me. Thank God spontaneous "things" do not fall from the sky; meteors, meteorites, and bird droppings are not spontaneous either by the way. If a ball of an unknown, purple gooey substance the size of a mini-van embedded with cheese and macaroni, a jet engine, and softballs were to suddenly appear on the 53rd floor of a skyscraper for no reason at all, then that would also be an example of spontaneous materialization. Things like this do not happen anywhere nor at any time, nor have they ever happened. Nothing spontaneously appears; automobiles, trains, boats, staplers, crayons, and whatever else do not just appear, and neither did human beings. People imagine objects first (note the root word, "image"), and then a process is begun to bring each object into physical existence. First, pictures may be drawn to represent spiritual objects, and then specific materials are gathered and manufactured to desired specifications to make those objects. Everything we physically make are representations of either individual or collective spiritual thoughts borne from perceived physical necessities and artistic desires. Every single thing in existence has many purposes.

Human beings are the spirit of man (which was created in the image and likeness of God) in individual physical bodies. When the spirit of man is joined with an individual human body, it then *becomes an individual, independent soul* (Genesis 2:7 KJV), and there is an ever-working double correlation between the spirit of man, and each person's body, both positive and negative. My individual soul (my personality, my will) controls my body, and I physically do whatever I individually spiritually **choose to do** in spite of contemporary spiritual and physical influences. This is what we call "behavior", and behaviors progressively manifest recognizable "personalities" from each body. Each person's behavior (manifested personality) eventually becomes recognizable as a pattern of conscious choices to everyone else.

We physically exist in this physical realm but make no mistake about it; this is a spiritual existence. After someone we know dies for example, we may indeed remember some physical characteristics about them, but we will mostly remember their spirit. We will remember the things they used to say and the way they said them for instance, or the way they behaved, talked, thought, etc.; the spiritual things about them. After someone dies, people worldwide (including atheists) naturally say things like, "Put the body over there.", or "His/her body looks good.", or "*That* didn't look like him/her.", or "His/Her body will lie in state...", and other similar expressions. All of these expressions naturally refer to the commonly understood *fact* that a dead body is just an "object" a person used to spiritually inhabit. We **all** naturally verbalize the fact that this is indeed a spiritual existence *through* a human body. We often hear sports announcers naturally talk about the competitive spirits of different teams and individual winners and champions, and anyone who participates in sporting events with any regularity already knows that competitiveness goes far beyond being just physical. The spiritual determination individual athletes compete with and against, as well as winning teams' indomitable, collective wills to win, are some identifiable realities of spiritual interactions in the sports arena.

Human bodies are physical and are therefore physically affected by functional realities in this physical realm such as time, nutrition and hydration, temperature, gravity, disease, physical activities (or lack thereof), and many other such variables. A person's body can be perfectly healthy and otherwise able to live, but **without its designated spirit in it**, that body is dead (like a parked car) because it has no personality; no operator; no spirit. Each of us is spiritually responsible for what our physical bodies do while we're in them, and we will be held individually accountable by God Almighty in the Name of Jesus Christ when our bodies die; and every(body) IS GOING TO DIE. Our bodies need to be serviced daily to work properly but regardless of what we do, the **human body** will no longer last more than 120 years in this physical realm because God said so (Genesis 6:3; KJV). How can that fact be otherwise explained? **Every** living thing in this physical realm dies. Why? Why does every living thing die? It is because we are existing in a physical realm which has a definitive beginning and a definitive end (because of sin), and therefore everything existing *within this finite realm* also (of course) HAS TO begin and end either before or when this entire physical realm does. We do not know the date of the beginning of this physical realm, nor do we know when it will end; but it has definitely begun, and it will definitely end (Romans 14:11, 12; 2 Peter 3:10; Acts 17:31 KJV).

Everything physical is subject to time because everything physical is in motion, and as explained in Chapter 2, *"Our Universe"*; physical motion and time are intricately connected. Time (as we know it) is a finite reality and **only** exists in this physical realm. Because time does not spiritually exist (in the realm of infinity), then there is no such thing as time to a dead person's spirit. If for example, a human being has been dead for 153 years, then the passage of time has only had a *physical* effect on their dead body (decomposition) because that body is still somewhere in this physical realm. Time ceased to exist for the spirit which used to consciously occupy that body 153 years ago however, because that soul immediately entered into the realm of infinity where there is no such thing as time as we know it. If that same spirit COULD consciously rejoin that same body which had been dead for 153 years (if it could be reconstituted right now in this physical realm), then "finite time" for that person would start up again from the exact moment of reconstitution, but that person would have no spiritual sense of how much time has physically gone by (153years) because they have not been subject to it. This is clearly and continuously evidenced by unconscious people's obliviousness to how much time has passed since they first became unconscious after they have regained consciousness. We ALL experience this paradigm of timelessness each time we go to sleep and wake up oblivious to the time which has gone by. This reality also fully explains the scriptures in the Holy Bible which refer to being absent from the body and being present with The Lord (2 Corinthians 5:6-10 KJV) as opposed to the dead in Christ rising first when He comes back (1 Thessalonians 4: 14-17 KJV).

Without being in a human body, our individual spirits cannot access this physical realm and this means that once our bodies die, our spirits are permanently separated from this physicality. There are no "*human* spirits" (ghosts) in this physical realm. There is The Holy Spirit of God, and there are evil, lying, confusion perpetuating demons.

Our physical bodies manifest our individual souls' spiritually requested actions as well as they are physically able to do, and the individual physical conditions of our bodies greatly influence how we interact with everything else physical; especially other people. "Awareness", or the phrase "to be aware of..." literally means *A person's sensitivity to the spirit realm in any given situation* although most contemporary definitions are worded differently because the spirit realm is rarely openly acknowledged in the world's sciences anymore. Anyway, I believe each person's sensitivity to the spirit realm (awareness) has the potential to be scientifically measured and that it varies significantly from person to person depending on different spiritual and physical variables.

When human beings are close to each other, our individual spirits interact while we are also interacting with good and evil spirits, and individuals' spiritual sensitivities are publicly discernible. We are continuously aware of other people's spiritual levels of awareness (some far more than others) because we spiritually communicate with each other all of the time. For example, if a sexually stimulated man in a nightclub is looking for a one night stand and he approaches a group of women seated at the bar, then his spirit is continually assessing their levels of spiritual awareness of his ultimate sexual intent based on their responses, actions, and reactions to his words and physical actions. He is spiritually looking for any individual sexual vulnerabilities any of the women may have which he can try to physically exploit. He is trying to spiritually discern if there are any of the women who are less spiritually aware of his goal (more naïve) than the others; which ones of them are not sexually interested in him at all; or if there are any who are willingly receptive to his intent. These are only some of the spiritual assessments he is making the entire time in this example and the description, "a wolf in sheep's clothing" may accurately describe some men in these kinds of situations.... women too for that matter!

People who are generally not as spiritually aware as they should be (regardless of the reasons), are more susceptible to people with bad intentions getting too close to them in vulnerable situations, and this increases their potential to become victims of otherwise avoidable crimes and negative situations. People's intentions, moods, desires, etc., either good or evil, ***can be*** spiritually discerned, and I tried to be especially spiritually aware of other people when I was a younger man because I was a black male growing up in a small, economically depressed town in southern America. When I would drive my car anywhere for example, I had to be continuously spiritually aware of not only potential car-jackers and other criminals looking for victims, but also of injudicious and racist law enforcement officers on duty because they existed aplenty during that time. I was stopped and had my license and registration checked without any probable cause many times. When I was 25 years old, I was arrested and put in jail for no reason at all after supposedly "fitting the description" of a rape suspect. Had I been more spiritually aware at the time, I would have immediately gotten back into my car and left the area from the very beginning of the situation. I was at a gas station in Columbia, South Carolina in 1989 at about 2am when I noticed a police car drive by the station and slow down. I saw the officer (who was a young, white male) look at me with a hateful look on his face, but I did not immediately spiritually discern the situation. I continued taking my time going in and out of the store, talking and joking around with the store clerks, and wiping and checking my car. A short while later, three police cars pulled into the station parking lot and as the officers (all of them white) got out of their cars, some of them pointed their guns at me and started yelling for me to hang up the pump and to keep my hands visible. The officers arrested me on suspicion of rape and then changed the story at the scene and said they were arresting me for driving while my license was suspended. Even if my license HAD BEEN suspended (and they had NOT been), I still wasn't "driving" when the officers came over to me from the beginning. They roughed me up a little and ended up taking me to jail at about 3am where I stayed until about 11:00am the following morning. I was not allowed to make a phone call the entire time, and my mother was in a hotel room waiting for me to return from the gas station the entire time. We had gone to Ft. Jackson, South Carolina to see my brother (her son) graduate from US Army Basic Training, and I had gone out that night to gas the car up ahead of time for the next day's drive back home after the ceremonies. I was a young Army officer (2LT) at the time, and my North Carolina Driver's License was indeed valid. The charges were later dropped and the case dismissed after I wrote a letter to that local District Attorney (D.A.) explaining what had happened. That incident made me want to become a police officer and I did so later that same year in Goldsboro, North Carolina.

I have been criminally victimized by other people as well and as a result, I have developed into an exceptionally spiritually sensitive and discerning middle aged adult. I believe a person's level of spiritual awareness is scientifically measurable, but the sleep-state of each person; the safety of the contemporary physical situation, each test subjects' will, and each test subjects' spiritual knowledge, as well as other less important variables, must all be considered. Sensitivity to the spirit realm is awareness, and the level of each person's spiritual awareness is lessened by physical attentional activities. Physical attentional activities are indicators of what we call *consciousness*, and a person is deemed to be conscious when they continuously display intentional acts of directing one or more of their senses to gather information from particular areas of interest (i.e. they are looking at something, listening to something, intentionally touching something, etc.). Some additional indicators of consciousness (and these are especially important when observing people with severe birth defects or other physically disabling challenges) are long-term, purpose driven attitudes and actions which when considered altogether, manifest as consistent personalities, and sensory perceptions (detectable/observable responses to different sensory stimulations).

During times of diminished physical attentional activities such as sleeping, comatose conditions, or even near-death experiences, our awareness of the spirit realm increases correlationally with the depths of our physical unconsciousness. Later on, after we've regained full physical consciousness, it is often difficult for people to put spiritual interactions into words, but s*ome* aspects of those interactions may sometimes be remembered and we call those "dreams". I will explain dreams more later on, but the spirit realm and the physical realm are interestingly separated and this separation is why we *do not* become super-aware of our physical realm atmospheres and locations once we become unconscious and are functioning spiritually.

We are individual human spirits continually in contact with The Holy Spirit as well as demonic spirits *through* our physical bodies. Physically perceivable **spiritual interactions** in this physical realm **only occur** in unique situations and circumstances such as miracles after righteous prayer, or signs and wonders associated with demonic activities. This entire physical realm is a sphere of spiritual influence when it comes to mankind and our individual bodies make it possible for our residing spirits to be able to be aware of other spirits also operating in this physical realm. We can be aware of someone else's physical presence in an area without actually seeing, hearing, or otherwise physically sensing that they are around us. People commonly say things like, "I don't know….I just had a feeling…", or "I sensed that someone was here.", or "I knew someone was watching me.", or "something told me to look for you over there.", etc. Sometimes we look in particular directions for no specific reasons and make direct eye contact with someone else looking at us.

I went back to college as an adult and I drove a full-sized Ford conversion, F-150 Econoline van with very dark tinted windows (limousine tint) all the way around with a curtain behind the front seats. If you didn't know I was in the back of that van, you would not have known I was sitting in one of those "captain's chairs" because you could not see into the van at all from the outside. I would park near particularly busy sidewalk areas on campus and sit in the back of the van in positions to observe thousands of ever-different college students and others continually walking by day after day. I knew for a fact that those people could not have seen me from any perspective up and down the entire length of those sidewalks because I always checked and made sure that I could not have been seen. I was only one of hundreds of vehicles parked along those roads each day and as I sat next to those sidewalks observing people day after day, so many different people made direct and extended eye contact with me that I had to get out of the van on several occasions to verify that they were not intentionally looking at me. It happened so often I began to think, "Well, even if they DO somehow know that I'm back here, they have no way of knowing where I am back here, so why do they keep making direct and extended eye contact with me?!" I KNEW that they could not have been seeing me. They were undoubtedly spiritually sensing my presence and obviously unbeknownst to them, making direct eye contact with me.

Sleep is an inevitable function of the physical body because the body needs to periodically rest and repair its physical components so it can continue to operate normally when it is conscious. Almost every day, we (our individual souls) position our bodies somewhere safe so we can intentionally diminish our physical attentional activities to the point that physical relaxation is possible and then we go to sleep. While someone is sleeping, the spirit in that body still functions just as it always does (your personality remains the same), only now there are greatly diminished physical attentional activities to impede spiritual interactions. Our spirits cannot completely leave our bodies or our bodies will die, so the freedom of the spirit is limited by the sleeping body because the physical condition of the body has to be continually "manned". This is evidenced by a sleeping person's awareness and recognition of temperature changes, uncomfortable body positions, unusual or unexpected sounds and movements in the immediate area, bathroom needs, etc. Sometimes when we sleep, spiritual interactions physically stimulate us and different kinds of dreams are examples of this. Remember, spiritual interactions are not always very accurately remembered after a person wakes up, but when we *can* recall aspects of those spiritual interactions, we call them dreams. We already know that most people do not often describe things they physically (consciously) witness as accurately as it would seem, so we can infer with confidence then, that people's descriptions of spiritual interactions are probably even less accurate. Soon after waking up, we seem to remember each dream like series of still photographs and we fill in the blank gaps between the "stills" as we describe dreams because we are attempting to make rational stories from them. Most of the "stills" fade from our conscious memories a short time later and we end up forgetting about most dreams. However; dreams sometimes physically stimulate brain neurons and cause physical reactions to occur and if most of us could have been observed while we were having those particular kinds of physically interactive dreams, we were probably swinging, smiling, masturbating, changing facial expressions, etc. If physical stimulation *does* occur during dreams, then those dreams are easier to remember because the physical memory cells in the brain relating to those physical actions were stimulated the exact same way they are when we are conscious. Remember, each one of us is the same personality (spirit) in dreams that we are when we're conscious and we interact with everything in those dreams the same way. It serves to reason that when we're physically stimulated during dreams, those dreams are easier to remember. The spirit (personality) residing in a body does not change because the body is sleeping or otherwise unconscious because we are infinite spirits residing in finite bodies, experiencing individual existences in this physical realm.

"Pay attention!" What do we actually mean when we tell someone else to pay attention? We are asking their soul to immediately refocus all of their available physical senses onto whomever, whatever, or wherever it is we desire. Who is it that is paying attention? Who is it making the decisions about where to look, what to listen to, and what to touch? It is your spirit/soul; your personality inside that body; you make those decisions. Some people say they do not believe there is a spirit realm at all. They do not want to believe that human beings are individual spirits in individual bodies but when those same people say, "I have a headache.", or "My knee hurts." for example, those are declarations which undoubtedly express possession, and possession in any circumstance requires two separate entities; there has to be "something", and then there has to be "something else" which realizes it "has" possession of that "something". Those are two different things. There absolutely **has to be** a separate, independent recognition of a body's condition in order for an individual person to be able to make any physical evaluations and comments about themselves such as, "*my* knee hurts". Well; whose knee is it? It is the spirit who is using that body, that's whose knee it is. "You" are in control of what "your" body does and every(body) is going to eventually die. After that happens, each of our spirits will be held individually accountable for what we have done and how we directed our bodies to operate while we were in them. This is like a car and its' driver. The driver is in complete control of what that car does and when there is a problem with the car, how does the driver express that? The driver (the "spirit" in that car) says for example, "I have a flat tire.", or "My battery is getting weak". Whether or not a driver drives dangerously, is speeding and running red lights, or is properly obeying the rules of the road, that driver is 100% responsible for how they directed that car to operate while they were in it.

Our attentional processes can also be *involuntarily refocused* by external stimuli such as unexpected sounds, loud noises, or sudden occurrences. In such situations, our bodies respond faster than our spirits can direct them to react and these are known as orientation responses. For example, if someone unexpectedly sets off a loud firecracker near your location, your body would most likely initially react by jumping and looking before your spirit could regain conscious control of your attentional processes. Before the firecracker went off, your spirit and body were focused on whatever it was you were doing and in the first instant after the explosion, your physical senses were involuntarily reoriented to the direction of the explosion. Your physical brain will not immediately decipher the instant flood of physical information from your different senses until you're able to spiritually regain control of your attentional processes (regain functional consciousness) which; depending on any resulting physical injuries and the individual involved, may take anywhere from a few seconds to much longer. This "reintegration process" is academically referred to as shock and the variability in times for reintegration happens for various reasons. Some of these reasons include age and other potentially limiting physical conditions, previous exposures and experiences, prior training, personal spiritual "intestinal fortitude", and other factors, which I will discuss in the next paragraph. Again, shock is occurring when the spirit is trying to reconnect with the physical body after a major involuntary refocusing or unexpected incident. Whatever you immediately heard, saw, felt, smelled, etc. regarding an involuntary refocusing incident (in this case, an unexpected firecracker explosion), is initially non-sensible to the brain especially if it is outside of the normal parameters of occurrences for that particular physical brain. A person who works in a place where firecrackers go off unexpectedly all the time for instance, would most likely have less of an orientation response to a firecracker unexpectedly exploding somewhere when they are not at work.

Our brains attempt to instantly, physically rationalize any sudden unexpected incidents while simultaneously managing our bodies' adrenal and physical responses. These tasks can sometimes be too much for the brain to instantly manage and when this happens, our spirits cannot access the normal neural pathways in the brain because although a person's spirit may have immediately recognized a sudden incident, their brain did not and was temporarily overloaded with trying to put everything in said physical perspective. The brain will eventually settle down and the spirit will then be able to re-access the normal neural pathways. This is why people can sometimes physically witness or be involved in traumatic incidents and then soon afterwards, not be able to describe what happened even though sometimes they may appear to experience the incident again and again. They are in shock. This reintegration process (shock) rectifies in varying amounts of time for each person and not only because of the previously mentioned reasons, but it also depends on the depth of spiritual control a person has over their physical body. For example, a person who is around dead bodies on a regular basis for whatever reasons would be far less likely to go into shock if they were unexpectedly exposed to a dead body, whereas a person who has never seen a dead body before at all would be more likely to go into a longer period of shock. Only "more likely" because people are very complex beings and everyone is capable of reacting differently than expected to any given situation. This is why we hear people say he/she "came back to their senses". Think about it, who is it that is coming back to monitor their senses?

We are each a human spirit contained in a human body which was born into sin and shaped in iniquity (Psalms 51:5; KJV), so there is a natural negative correlation between the human body and The Holy Spirit, and a natural positive correlation between the human body and demonic spirits. Our bodies are literally made of defiled physical matter (dirt from the Earth) and it has all been scheduled for destruction by Almighty God; its Creator, because of sin. We are in an atmosphere where spiritual and physical sin exists, and every conscious person at any given point in time is consistently manifesting behaviors influenced by a percentage combination of both physical and spiritual variables; both good and evil. Some of the **physical variables** include the contemporary physical environment, the physical situations and circumstances, and the physical health of an individual. The physical ability to *manifest* behaviors is different in each body due to individual genetics, physical body damage, etc. **Spiritual variables** include encouraging and discouraging influential spirits, both good and evil. *Influential spirits* are either Holy (righteous), or demonic (evil), and each human soul makes final determinations as to which behaviors they ultimately consciously decide to express. In cases of reprobation (no more *righteous* spiritual suggestions from God resulting from too many prior negative decisions), we are still certainly responsible for our ultimate behaviors because our prior decisions caused the reprobate condition to exist in the first place. I will talk more about reprobation in Chapter 5: *"THE PHYSICALITY OF REPROBATE PERCEPTIONS"*.

We are each spiritual beings experiencing this physical realm through a physical body, and if we can intentionally pay attention to anything physical with any of our senses, then we are alive and conscious and our bodies are at least somewhat functional. Sometimes when people's bodies have been severely physically damaged, their spirits are not able to override the physical conditions of their bodies and they can *only try* to physically express themselves. This is similar to someone driving a car with a clogged catalytic converter. A clogged catalytic converter makes a car operate sluggishly so the driver of that car may intend to keep up with other vehicles and function just as quickly as they do, but the manifestations of the driver's intended actions are obviously severely restricted because of the clogged converter. His or her intended motions physically manifest much slower than other drivers on the road the same way a physically challenged person's actions are slower and different when compared to a healthy person's actions. Our bodies require spiritual energy to operate and the manifestation of people's spiritual expressions through their bodies is influenced greatly by at least *three major* factors; the physical condition of the senses (eyes, ears, skin condition, etc.), the body's contemporary location (am I in physical danger? ...do I need to look, listen, run, etc.?), and personal spiritual desires (concentrating on lustfully *looking* at him or her, rather than *listening* to what he or she is saying) for example.

The Breath of Life/Spirit of Man is the same amount of spiritual energy in every living human being and that energy is manifested through each physical body differently depending on each body's physical capabilities. The amount of spiritual energy inhabiting each living body (the spiritual life force) does not change throughout a human life cycle, but our physical bodies do. The *capabilities* of each human body are physically different because of genetics, exercise, the cumulative foods and water they have consumed over time, particular atmospheric compositions, injuries, deformities, etc., and our bodies progressively require more and more spiritual energy to operate as we age. While human beings are children, the amount of physical energy needed to operate our little bodies is dwarfed by the amount of spiritual energy available to us. We are born with enough spiritual energy to power an adult and little bodies get tired quickly because they are spiritually "overpowered", so to speak. This is the reason babies become quickly exhausted and sleep so much, and also why small children stay awake for as long as they can until they literally collapse in place. Spiritual energy starts out being too much for our little bodies but as we grow, our physical cells require more and more spiritual energy to operate until eventually physical energy demands begin to compete with the supply of spiritual energy available to us. At different times in each of our lives, our available spiritual energy and our physical energy requirements "equalize" for a period of time. This is the athletic/energetic prime period in males and females alike and this normally occurs somewhere between the ages of 23 and 50. The duration of this period for each person depends heavily on those previously mentioned *physical* variables such as genetics, exercise, cumulative food and water intakes, etc. After this spiritual/physical equilibrium period has passed, staying fully alert all day long becomes more and more of a physical challenge, and this is why adults physically *recharge* themselves with caffeine drinks and other physical stimulants while those same stimulants will "overcharge" children. As we continue to age beyond the athletic/energetic prime period, our desires to be extracurricularly active such as the willingness to jump around, aggressively dance, the desire to run, the determination to play, etc., lessen more and more as time continues, because that "extra" spiritual energy is now limited by the fact that the body needs that same energy more and more for basic operations. Extra activities become mostly unnecessary energy-burning operations, so we naturally change our personal physical priorities. This change is good because our bodies become progressively weaker and more apt to injuries as we age. Caffeine drinks and other stimulants help adult bodies be more physically able to manifest spiritually desired behaviors for longer periods of time, but older bodies can sometimes physically manifest different behaviors than the residing spirit intended because of natural physical deteriorations or damage to the body. The human body is physical and will naturally develop various problems due to deteriorations over time such as Alzheimer's Disease, broken hips and bones, etc. There is a spiritual realm and there is a physical realm, and *only in human beings* is this combination manifested as self-conscious, self-aware individuals who are each spiritually aware of (sensitive to) good and evil spirits through a physical body. We are conscious, spiritual beings living in temporary bodies in a temporary physical realm. What is physical consciousness? Physical consciousness is attentional awareness; *an individual spirit's ability to use its body's senses.* We can, and have used our bodies' senses to investigate God's creation (this universe) since we have existed and in the next chapter, Chapter 2; *"OUR UNIVERSE"*, I will explain some of what we think we have scientifically learned.

(CHAPTER TWO)

OUR UNIVERSE

The contemporary worldwide public should be aware that many modern influential scientists are **interpreting** experimental conclusions and scientific observations almost exclusively through a big bang, evolutionary filter. God created this universe/time (Colossians 1:16-17 KJV, John 1:1-5; KJV, Isaiah 48:12,13 KJV) and based on The Holy Bible and any scientific evidence human beings have ever studied, we do not know when that happened. It could have been billions of years ago or it could have been thousands of years ago; none of us know for sure. "Time" is a *physical* variable because there is a definitive beginning to this physical existence, and a predetermined end to everything as well (Jesus returns and the world comes to an end). Since this entire physical universe (everything in existence) has a definitive beginning and a definitive end, then of course everything existing *within* the universe **must** have (and of course, to a lesser extent) a beginning and an end. This is why nothing here lasts forever (everything starts, begins, or is born, and then everything ends, stops and dies). This reality also makes it possible for us to physically measure time because there are spans of *measurable* moments *within* this universe in which motion takes place, and the speed of that motion (from beginning to end) will determine the "time" (culmination of the spans of moments) it takes for that motion to have occurred from start to finish. The *passage* of time in this physical realm is a micro/macro continuous reality of forces in motion, and every physical thing in existence is in coordinated motion at the molecular level with everything else physical; therefore, motion is the *fabric* of physical relativity or time. What is this temporary physical realm (the universe)? The universe is everything in physical existence everywhere, including all life forms. It is a compilation of continuously interacting physical forces partially manifested as mass, operating in a seemingly endless open vacuum, and since we can **physically** sense (i.e. see, hear, measure, detect, etc.) the sun, other moons, galaxies, planets, other distant stars, etc., then the universe is physical and is therefore finite.

Human beings can recognize and appreciate the glories of the universe because *the universe was created by God* **for** *us*; to contain us. It takes a place this large and complex to contain a planet full of human beings. Think about how much we each already know about everything and how much more we each have the potential/capacity to know. For example, the topics I'm discussing right now you can understand while at the same time there are literally millions of different things around you wherever you are right now that you know all kinds of things about. Think about how many people you know; their names and what they each look and sound like, past and present. Think about all the memories you have about all the individual people and all of the different incidents, sounds, situations, circumstances, etc., you and others have experienced. Think about all the places we each are familiar with, and all the different arts, songs, colors, the different sports, statistics, smells, all of the directions to so many different places (driving, walking, jogging, biking, air, sea, etc.), all of the academics (math, science, history, languages, etc.), past and current friends and enemies, fashions, the planets, cooking, space, songs, talents, your jobs (past and present), emotions, prices, tools, sex, and on, and on. Think about "numbers". Each number is represented by a physical mark which stands for a different, God-assigned segment of the entire structure of this physical realm. For example, if I say to you that 2+2=4, then you know exactly what that means and you can apply it in numerous ways to various things although I transferred nothing physical to you. Numbers look and sound different in every language human beings use, yet each number still represents the same unique, spiritually predetermined segment or amount of space, time, and calculatable portions of anything physical in this physical realm to us. The values are the same and mean the same thing to each and every human being regardless of what we call each number (as do fish). What does that mean? It means that God in The Name of Jesus Christ by His Holy Spirit established the spiritual, foundational structure of numbers (and everything else as well) so that we can understand physicality. Without standard, applicable, numerical representations (numbers) representing segments of this physically manifested spiritual structure (the physical realm), then it would be impossible for us to understand anything about the brilliance of God's physical purposes and His design structures which carry them out.

We are tiny physical organisms, yet we understand so much. We have indeed been created in the image and likeness of Almighty God and we are as improbable as microscopic bits of bacteria on my left kneecap for example, understanding where they are in relation to the rest of my body as well as other intimate details about my body's entire physical composition. That bacteria would understand facts like there are other human bodies and how differently each one looks, how they move, the sun and the moon's movements, and a myriad of other incredibly accurate facts about its physically insignificant, yet spiritually aware existence. That bacteria would be comparable to humanity. No, human beings are not spontaneous results of random happenstance; that is absolutely and demonically ridiculous. Each one of us is a special individual with divine purposes for existing. We are spiritual images of Almighty God contained in tiny physical bodies, and we each have access to His Nature and Being through Jesus Christ by His Holy Spirit. There are *billions* of little images of Almighty God alive on this Earth in human bodies at any given point in time, so of course it takes an intricately micro-macro detailed (tiny - large scale) universe like this to contain us. Yes, as far as humanity and organic life is concerned, we are alone in this universe.

Within this universe, God placed us on planet Earth and this earth is part of a "solar system" (a bunch of rocks and gas and stuff going around a star) which is estimated to be over 7 billion miles wide…an almost unimaginable distance. To be more descriptive, a solar system is made up of a star in the middle (like our sun) with planets (some gas and some rocky) and other large matter spinning around that particular star. In our solar system, there are at least eight planets orbiting around our sun as well as other large rocks, dirt, ice chunks, etc. We call our star "The Sun", and it theoretically figures to last for at least 15 billion more years. It is only one of several hundred million stars in our galaxy, and the sun is very hot. The average temperature across the surface of the sun at any given time is about 7,600 degrees Fahrenheit (F). There are "cooler" areas on the surface of the sun which randomly appear and disappear in different locations and we call these "sunspots". The sunspots we have been able to study, range in temperature from around 4,600 degrees F at the "coolest", to around 7,500 degrees F. Because these small, rounded areas are cooler, they appear darker than the sun's surrounding surface areas and every 11 or so years these sunspots increase in number and cause a very slight decrease in the sun's overall temperature by roughly 1/10th of 1 degree. This ever so slight temperature change significantly affects the Earth's weather and its magnetosphere (causing different kinds of storms as well as more visible Aurora Borealis mostly near the Earth's polar regions). We are approximately 93 million miles from our sun and it takes light from the sun between 7 and 8 minutes to reach the Earth even though it is travelling about 186,000 miles each second.

A galaxy is a gathering of billions of individual stars and solar systems arranged in recognizable shapes in space including spiral, elliptical, lenticular/barred, and some other irregular patterns and shapes as well. Most of the stars and suns in *each* galaxy are at least millions of light years away from each other, and we've concluded that our sun is located somewhere in a relatively small spiral shaped galaxy of stars we've named, "The Milky Way Galaxy". If we were to get into a vehicle and travel at the speed of light (again moving at about 186,000 miles *each second*), it would still take us *at least 100,000 years* just to cross the Milky Way. In **one year** alone, light travels about **6 trillion** miles.

The Milky Way Galaxy is only one galaxy of stars in the entire universe and like grains of sand on a beach, they are practically impossible to number; there are trillions of individual galaxies. Many individual galaxies seem to be grouped into clusters of what appear to be multi-millions and *each cluster* of galaxies is only one cluster in a group of *billions* of other galaxy clusters. Furthermore, the galaxy clusters seem to be grouped into *galaxy super-clusters*, and it literally seems to be endless. The size of this universe is beyond our ability to calculate because we know that it continues far beyond what we can see and detect with any of our most advanced scientific instruments. Also, our best mathematical calculations regarding the entire size of this universe seem to come back around onto themselves without any tangible conclusions. What we know right now is that there are at the very least, many trillions of galaxies in this universe and that each galaxy contains at least one hundred thousand, million stars. Any historically anecdotal information using any kind of configuration which represents a "calculated size of the universe" for **any** "scientific" conclusion can ONLY be pure circumstantial speculation. Atheistic modern scientists commonly use this kind of information to bolster their Godless theories as to how we exist.

How do we know to challenge our children by *allowing them* to explore atmospheres we have intentionally designed for them such as baby cribs with mobiles, bedrooms with puzzles, games, maps, and all other kinds of different toys? We lovingly organize stimulating teaching environments and consistently allow our children to recognize and discover age appropriate realities. God is how we already know what to do in order to teach our children because this is how He teaches us. Humans have always been curious about this universe (2 Kings 23:5 KJV) and there will always be something else to learn as long as this physical realm exists because there are at least positive, negative, and neutral forces continuously *in motion* which make up everything physical. Motion is therefore, a physical property that *everything* in this physical realm shares, and this means that everything in this physical realm has a force-relationship (to almost infinitely varying degrees) with everything else in this physical realm. Some other common properties of everything physical include the fact that everything has a temperature; the fact that everything is a particular distance away from everything else; the fact that everything suffers from physical disintegrations due to the passage of time; and other properties of that nature. Because motion is a common property in everything physical both micro and macro, I believe the actual motions of comets, moons, stars, planets, galaxies, dark matter and energy, and other forces out in space, are all inter-connectedly geared together in the ultra-magnetic, electro-chemical, gravitational vacuum of deep space. They all affect each other. God has perfectly coordinated this machine we call the universe.

Our sun expels solar winds, magnetic waves, photons, electromagnetic radiation, electricity, heat, rays, etc., out into space at all times and in every direction, yet at the same time we think the sun's gravitational "pull" holds all of the planets (including the little rock Pluto) and other even more distant bodies in stabilized orbits around it. For instance, it takes over three hours moving at the speed of light (just over 186,000 miles **each second**) to get to Pluto from the sun. The gravitational pull of the sun alone is unlikely to be able to be strong enough to hold objects in orbits from those extreme distances (at least 2,858,307,484 miles) while at the same time not sucking Mercury, Venus, and the Earth into itself. There are obviously other forces which we have not yet discovered which are keeping the sun's orbiting matter from either being sucked into it (dark matter or dark energy perhaps?), or from being slung out into open space. Modern scientists estimate that the universe is approximately 13.7 billion years old because of light speed calculations based on theoretical distances to a theoretical edge of the universe from the earth's perspective. That radius is then doubled to theoretically account for a complete "universal bubble" if you will. This age estimation of the universe is derived from light we can detect from the farthest light sources in deep space we can see or otherwise detect from the Earth and the theoretical time it would have taken that light to have gotten here from those extreme locations. If we calculate the distance of a point of light from us based on how long it theoretically took the light to get to us from that point of light, then the point of light would have had to have been placed where it is first, and then the light began travelling towards us. Only then could that calculation even possibly be valid. If a spontaneous big bang had occurred, then the light from the manifested matter would never have faded from the Earth's point of view since it theoretically began from the same place we did. The light would not have retracted itself from us and then started back towards us later on after the matter got to wherever it was going. Right now our skies would still be completely white with light from big bang astronomical mass "creation" had a big bang occurred. Some modern atheists claim that materialized matter from the big bang has remained still since the time it "spontaneously occurred" and that is still being pushed away from each other by the space in between (even though there are galaxies "colliding", meteors regularly smash into other planetary bodies, comets are circulating, etc.). God *placed* matter in the universe where and how He wanted it to be, and He then set all of the physical processes in motion. Studying the universe verifies exactly that. The "fear" (respect) of The Lord is the beginning of wisdom (Proverbs 1:7; 9:10 KJV), (Psalm 111:10 KJV) and people disrespect God every single time they foolishly ascribe His glorious masterpiece (this universe) to some "lucky spontaneous occurrence" which also supposedly spontaneously produced higher and more intelligent life forms than human beings (aliens). That didn't happen. God Is Almighty whether we CHOOSE TO physically acknowledge that fact or not, and if you believe there are other life forms which are smarter than humans in existence (if you believe in "UFOs, then you believe that), then you are declaring that there is someone higher and smarter than God since He created us in His very image and likeness. IT IS IMPOSSIBLE FOR GOD TO LIE and there are very negative consequences for believing demonic foolishness! You have your own brain and a free will. If you have convinced yourself that there is no God at all, then you're saying that spontaneity (which is *the opposite* of purpose) produced intelligent and intricately designed life forms in a physical realm in which we factually know that **everything** functions with purpose. That is impossible. Everything in this universe was created FOR human beings, and nothing in this physical realm is superior to us…..nothing.

"The Beginning", as it refers to the start of the previously described universe, is when God initiated physical motion. Remember, motion is common to everything physical because everything physical is in motion at the molecular/subatomic level at varying speeds. People who study mass at the molecular level, believe that atoms are tiny individual collections of particularly arranged positive, negative, and neutral forces, and that *the amount* of each force present in each atom determines what kind of physical element (matter) each atom will help to manifest when it's combined with other like atoms. We think that weak atomic combinations of these forces manifest soft matter such as cotton, feathers, grass, etc., while tighter/stronger combinations of those same forces (covalent bonds for example) help manifest hard matter such as rocks, iron, diamonds, etc. Again, atoms are believed to be tiny collections of positive, negative, and neutral forces, and there are theoretically multi-trillions of atoms making up any small area of anything physical. If matter is composed of combined forces of energy (atoms), then theoretically we should be able to make existing matter disappear or fall apart by dis-integrating the specifically integrated atomic bonds which make up that matter, and then seemingly make that same matter reappear by pressuring those same dis-integrated atoms back together (re-integrating them) at predictable pressures. When/if we develop this ability, then the modern scientific community would undoubtedly try to use that discovery/ability to further disrespect God by then claiming that this proves that matter was spontaneously manifested …..even though there is NOTHING spontaneous about what I've just described. The atoms have already been created and combined in each form of matter as per God's desires, and there is nothing spontaneous about any natural or man-made process which separates or combines any atom. Mankind's attempts to prove a spontaneous beginning is one of the motivations behind the building of the very expensive "CERN", the French acronymic name (European Organization for Nuclear Research) of a High-Energy Particle Accelerating Machine which was built underground in Switzerland. The CERN is basically a very large airtight tube approximately 17 miles in circumference and buried about 574 feet underground. This extremely large, multi-billion dollar underground tube is packed full of extremely powerful and intricately sensitive electromagnetic configurations which are used to accelerate molecular forces close to the speed of light, then smash them together for the purpose of discovering a "Higgs-Boson". This is supposedly a "God-particle" which helped *spontaneously* initiate the first physical matter, and it was reportedly discovered at the CERN sometime in 2012. This "particle" has (of course) not been scientifically shown to have spontaneously initiated anything and that's because it did not happen. To put it simply, the "Higgs-Boson" is an inevitable "must" which absolutely "HAD" to mathematically exist in order to physically (and errantly) validate any and all theories about the existence of this physical reality without it having been created. Regardless of what is **_ever_** discovered during the CERN acceleration-collision studies or at any other modern scientific facility or platform, including the James Webb and Edwin Hubble space telescope observations, we will ALWAYS only discover that everything has obviously been designed, and that God is THE DESIGNER.

It takes a "room" the size of this universe to contain human beings and in Chapter 3, *"SCIENTIFIC CONFUSION vs. THE TRUTH ABOUT THE UNIVERSE AND ORGANIC EXISTENCES"*, I will go into some details about why modern scientific confusion occurs when trying to atheistically explain the universe.

(CHAPTER THREE)

SCIENTIFIC CONFUSION VS. THE TRUTH ABOUT THE UNIVERSE AND ORGANIC EXISTENCES

What is "Science"? Science is a method we use to professionally investigate physical variables God has created in order for us to come to reliable conclusions about them. Human beings have come to scientific conclusions about many things over time, but our *interpretations* of the results of scientific experiments are subjective. This is an inherent problem. The following steps are a basic universal description of the scientific method: 1.) Observe the curiosity to be tested; 2.) Formulate questions and hypotheses to be answered about the curiosity; 3.) Predict what the answers will be to those questions; 4.) Gather the equipment and data for experimentation; 5.) Test/Experiment; 6.) Accept or reject the hypotheses and document the procedures and findings to allow for experimental replication for validation of the results.

Experimental results are interpreted by individuals (subjective), and modern scientists generally interpret scientific results through a predominately atheistic filter. This has unfortunately resulted in a lot of influential *modern scientists* presenting **intentionally misleading** "scientific" conclusions to the public which are motivated by a big bang/evolutionary agenda. This is one of the causes of existing animosities between "the church" and "science". The spontaneous big bang explanation for the beginning of everything (including life) is by far the most prominent example of the modern scientific community aggressively and intentionally presenting false conclusions to the world in the name of "science". Modern scientists study physicality in detail, but seem to have no interest in the spiritual truth about that same physicality. Studying physical facts helps us better understand physicality, but without understanding that the physical realm was indeed created, then understanding the *truth* about physical facts is not possible. Remember, "science" is only a *physical system* we use so that we can better understand physical facts, but **the reality of the spirit realm and creation** is literally **the interpretation** of physical facts. It takes faith to believe that God created the physical universe, but it takes FAR MORE FAITH to believe in a spontaneous happenstance purposeless beginning and existence because of the multi-trillions of super-intricate purposes for (every)thing which exists. Spontaneous happenstance means that things begin and exist for no reason and without interlocking purposes. Things came from nowhere and are just here serving no purposes.

God clearly created every ingredient which makes up the physical universe (Genesis, Hebrews 11:3; KJV), but God; The Almighty Creator, is rarely acknowledged if at all in contemporary science. This **modern idea** of excluding God from anything scientific is perpetuated by a confused adherence by the scientific community to a demonically inspired **intentional misapplication** of the United States' Constitution's meaning of "Separation of Church and State". The First Amendment to the United States Constitution literally states that "Congress shall make no law respecting an establishment of religion, or prohibiting the free exercise thereof; or abridging the freedom of speech, or of the press; or the right of the people peaceably to assemble, and to petition the government for a redress of grievances." As far as "separation of church and state" is concerned, the First Amendment only means that the government of the United States of America will not make any "religious" laws, nor will the American government dictate anything to anyone about who they worship and how they do it. I do think however, that The First Amendment to the U.S. Constitution needs this addition after "….the free exercise thereof;"; *unless obviously physically harmful (or otherwise criminal) religious requirements directly resulting in admittance to a hospital are involved with that "worship".* Perhaps that **meaning** will be added some day but nevertheless, the First Amendment to The United States Constitution has NOTHING at all to do with any civilian scientists acknowledging God in his/her scientific research. The First Amendment is specifically directed towards congressional legislation and this needs to be understood.

If modern scientists from any discipline include anything about God in any of their research explanations or conclusions, then the information is "professionally disregarded" by the modern scientific community citing "Separation of Church and State", and government and other funding is then almost always immediately discontinued. One of the unfortunate results of that has been interpretational confusion when it comes to trying to understand and explain experimental results. Physical sciences can only investigate tangible variables and cannot directly test spiritual variables, but the modern scientific community *should* make a better effort to develop experimentation which investigates spiritual influences in human circumstances. Spiritual experimentation is difficult to perform, but intricate spiritual influences in our physical circumstances are an absolute fact in this life. As I explain later in Chapter 3, *"Modern Science: Spirit Realm Research"*, the challenge is to gather valid experimental test subjects so as to ensure test-result validity.

Physical sciences have always verified The Holy Bible, and the fact that human beings naturally/physically resist acknowledging the obvious Truth of God in Jesus' Name is solid proof that we are spirits of God Almighty, born into a body literally ***made from*** this demonically defiled physical earth which has already been sentenced to eternal damnation. There is an evil, lying, spirit of the anti-Christ in existence (the devil) continuously negatively influencing each of our spirits. This naturally agrees with our already negatively defiled physical bodies and this is why we naturally have a positive correlation with evil, and why we each need the salvation of Jesus Christ. We are naturally intelligent enough to know that God is, and that He absolutely HAS to be! When spiritual and physical facts are presented to people who are certainly intelligent enough to understand them, yet they continuously position themselves against those truths, then there HAS TO BE a negative spiritual influence behind that position, otherwise …. why else would it happen?

Each of us spiritually know that anything *physical* can be manipulated (changed, defiled, deformed, rearranged, made better or worse, etc.), so we make stuff out of the physical things God has already created. All of God's organic creations (life forms) **make** things from what God has already ***created***, and to **"create"** something literally means to make something out of nothing. To **"make"** something means to take already created elements and change them. Simply stated, God ***created*** the universe and every ingredient in it (including life) ONE TIME and since then, the passage of physical time (motion) and God's created organisms have **made** things by changing and combining the variables which God has already created. Complicated, precisely organized, and extremely mathematically perfect and chemically balanced physical existences which could only have been "created" are everywhere at all times in micro, as well as macro forms.

Scientists are convinced that the universe is expanding based on astronomical observations and different tracking systems in different places on (this round) Earth which seem to indicate that everything in space is accelerating away from everything else. This entire universe is encapsulated by Spiritual Infinity, and the Bible refers to space as "the heaven", or "heavens" in various places. For instance, Psalms 8:1; KJV states, "O Lord our Lord, how excellent is thy name in all the earth! Who has set thy glory ***above*** the heavens". This tells us that God is bigger than the farthest of the heavens, and of course this is true because He created everything. It seems logical that the border/edge of the universe is the edge of physicality and where this physical realm meets God's Pure Spiritual Glory (Infinity). God is everywhere at the same time, and He always has been. Again, stars and other physical matter in deep space appear to be moving away from us as well as away from each other from any perspective here on earth. The earth is round, and if everything in deep space is moving away from us from every observation point on this round ball, then the Earth absolutely

HAS TO BE physically located in the center of the universe. God placed the stars and other physical matter in space where they are and set them in motion, and one of the most interesting things He did was to include big-bang/evolutionary "impossibilities". He did these things because He knew exactly what the spirit of the anti-Christ was going to try to do in the gullible and sinful minds of modern man. For instance, the planet Neptune's largest moon (Triton) orbits Neptune in the opposite direction from the rotation of the planet (a retrograde orbit which causes heat producing drag and friction), yet that particular moon is still the **coldest matter** in the solar system. There are *many more* moons around Neptune and other planets in this solar system which orbit their planets in opposite directions as well, and none of these would have been spontaneously possible at all by the laws of physics and quantum mechanics which we know exist and which we know govern physical relationships of matter. God is. The planet Uranus is positioned on its "side" and is rotating sideways in relationship to its orbit around the sun. It's "North Pole" is pointing at the sun. There are trillions of spontaneous beginning "impossibilities" God has designed into this universe and most of them are obvious; like matter in deep space moving faster and faster for instance. If we could watch this solar system from above, we would see that all of the planets are going around the sun (orbiting) in a counter-clockwise direction. The *individual rotations* of each planet are also counter-clockwise, as if they are rolling around the sun......with the exceptions of two very different planets; one of them very large and far away from the sun, while the other planet is small and extremely close. The planets "Uranus" and "Venus" are rotating clockwise. *A spontaneous happening* cannot explain these anomalies, and they do not fit into the laws of physics and quantum mechanics. God did it.

Some modern scientists foolishly theorize that the universe spontaneously began as some kind of energy tinier than the pointed end of a sewing needle, and that this imaginary particle supposedly somehow held temperatures and/or electrical/KW properties of more than one billion, billion degrees Fahrenheit. Supposedly it exploded about 10 to 15 billion years ago with a big bang; hence the name of the theory. These scientists commonly theorize that from that point the universe quickly expanded and after only a few seconds, it was already the size of this solar system (about 2,858,307,484 miles wide) and had cooled down to about 10 billion degrees. If this hogwash was even remotely true, then the universe would still be slowing down and cooling off, or at least still be expanding at the same rate and maintaining a constant temperature; only it isn't. The universe is instead manufacturing all kinds of heat everywhere and is in fact, speeding up! Atheists say that time, matter, energy, and space began with that spontaneous big bang, but if there were no such things as time, matter, energy, and space *before* this explosion, then there would not have been a **moment** for the explosion to have taken place, nor would there have been **anywhere** for it to have happened. **What was it composed of** if there were no such things as energy and matter? God has always been and God will always be, and the only explanation for everything IS creation.

Atheists conjure up ideas such as sister universes, alternating dimensions, fantasy worm-hole theories, etc., to try and imply that physical time, energy, matter, and space have always existed. None of this is true and there is not one shred of scientific evidence to support ANY of these conjured up theories, so don't believe the hype. It didn't happen. Big bang theorists are forced to support the idea that about 500,000 years after a spontaneous initial explosion, free particles *spontaneously* came into existence, followed by Hydrogen and Helium atoms (because this is the only way it could have spontaneously happened). This is absurd because even the most basic molecules we are aware of are far too complex and *undeniably purposefully* **designed** to produce the specific elements they produce, to have spontaneously formed on their own. God created free particles and every single building block of each and every chemical element as intricately and as precisely as He did so that man would have no excuse not to believe that God is. No sane person anywhere would look at a racing car's engine for example, and believe that the engine manufactured its own parts and then put itself together. *Each* molecule of each element, each gene, each chromosome, each neuron, each atom, and all the way down to the tiniest physical particle, is **far more** complicated than the most complicated engines in existence. How much more ridiculously blasphemous can mankind get…..and more importantly, how much more disrespect will God tolerate?

Regardless of their states of being (solid, liquid, gas, plasma, etc.), hydrogen is still hydrogen, nitrogen is still nitrogen, oxygen is still oxygen, and so on with all of the other elements. We can make accurate and reliable predictions about each chemical's behavior as well as their reactions to other chemicals under variable conditions because God created each element to be what it is, and elements do not spontaneously change. For example, we can make millions of plastic jars of different tasting peanut butters because we KNOW that if we mix particular ingredients together in particular ways with particular amounts of each ingredient, then unique tasting peanut butters as well as solid, clear, plastic jars to put them in will reliably result. We can put different kinds of peanut butter in manufactured jars *knowing with confidence* that there will be no cross-contamination from the jars, and that the jars will not disintegrate. How is this common process possible if chemical elements are only the results of lucky spontaneous happenings at the atomic level? Each chemical, molecule, atom, force, etc., could not maintain stable and reliable properties over time if they were only happenstance. They would not remain stable because they would spontaneously change every now and then on their own, and each jar of the exact same brand of peanut butter would have its own taste and flavor. Sometimes the jars would hold the peanut butter, and sometimes they would not because the plastic would sometimes disintegrate and melt into the peanut butter (if it was still peanut butter because the ingredients are subject to spontaneously change at any given moment). For instance, the jars, the labels on the jars, or the peanut butter in the jars could catch on fire at any time because of spontaneous chemical changes. If our existences were only spontaneous happenstances, then there would be no way for us to know *anything* physical with certainty. Because God created each element's complicated atomic structure to consistently maintain its properties, then we are able to know for instance, that liquid Oxygen will react violently with liquid Hydrogen every single time. God has always known exactly what He is doing. It is not possible for spontaneous happenstance to produce predictable consistency because it has no purpose, and every single thing here has many purposes.

Atheists say that as the universe continued to spontaneously expand, hydrogen and helium atoms luckily formed huge gas clouds and in these clouds, billions of unimaginably complex stars and galaxies took shape and then clustered themselves together. Within each galaxy, stars and planets decided to form and then gather themselves into complex, organized orbits, rotations, and movements. Not only did the galaxies decide to form into shapes and patterns recognizable to us, but nebulae, quasars, pulsars, and all kinds of other matter also decided they would form on their own. There are many recognizable shapes in deep space like spirals, a horse's head, a ring, a crab, a hand, a soccer ball, and many more. These shapes and patterns are millions and sometimes multi-billions of light years away from us, yet they are easily recognizable and identifiable to us as common shapes and objects. It cannot have been spontaneous.

Modern scientists say the earth then "formed" and *positioned itself* perfectly far enough away from the sun for everything to start working perfectly on its own by tilting itself 23 degrees towards the sun, then settling itself into a *perfect* rotation and orbit speed so that days, years, seasons, water, etc. could exist. The moon then suddenly *somehow* appeared (there is no "scientific" explanation for the moon) and then things just….. started living on the Earth. This entire thought process is ridiculous. Even the tiniest changes in positional relationships between the Earth, the moon, or the sun would produce immediate and catastrophic devastation to all life on Earth and probably the Earth itself. Everything would freeze, burn up, float off into space, or die in a poisoned, magnetic, electrified atmosphere. God positioned the moon at such an exact distance between the Earth and the sun, that right now it **perfectly** eclipses the sun so that only the sun's outer atmosphere (corona) is visible all the way around during an eclipse. Spontaneous happenstance? No. Our moon rotates on its axis approximately once every 27 days and at the same time, the moon orbits the earth approximately once every 27 days in an oval pattern. God perfectly coordinated the moon's rotation, orbit, and other forces to cause the same side of the moon to face the earth at all times, and we call this tidal synchronization. God placed the earth and the moon in an intricately coordinated relationship with each other, and try to imagine the complication involved in creating two round, differently sized balls levitating in a most extremely hostile and lifeless atmosphere, with each ball having an independent sphere of gravity. He independently spun them at different rates of rotation and made the smaller ball orbit around the larger one and positioned everything so that the sun is perfectly and predictably eclipsed by the smaller ball (the moon) when viewed from the larger ball's (the earth) perspective. The smaller ball also causes various changes on the surface of the larger ball, most notably critical oceanic tides. Hallelujah!! God Is Supreme Intelligence far beyond what we can even begin to comprehend! The moon produces tides in the oceans and seas all over the world while appearing from the Earth to be in different phases (full, half, new, etc.) as it orbits the Earth because of both planets' continuously changing positional relationships to the sun. The moon's effects occur so regularly that we produce dependable schedules and calendars from them. Interestingly enough, the moon is also moving away from the earth at a little more than an inch per year, and that back-calculates to the moon being in contact with the Earth anywhere between 7000 and 13,000 years ago (allowing for motion variations and other possible anomalies). The moon is only about 238,900 miles from the Earth, and atheists have no explanation for its existence except to say that maybe an asteroid about the size of Mars (it would have to have been) struck the earth sometime in the past and knocked a chunk out into space and then this chunk supposedly became the moon. There are just *too many* reasons why this theory is ridiculously absurd. Some modern scientists also try to say the moon just happened to be floating through the solar system on its own and accidentally got caught up in the Earth's gravitational pull after it got too close……anyway; enough of that foolishness. The existences of any of the moons around any of the planets cannot be explained without God having created them. They are each characteristically very different even when they are orbiting the same planets. There are 181 moons that we know of orbiting the eight (8) large planets and (5) five smaller "dwarf planets" in our solar system. Obviously some of the planets have many moons in orbit around them, but some of them have none. Mercury, Venus, the Earth, and Mars are considered to be "terrestrial planets" and Mercury and Venus have no moons, while the Earth has one and Mars two. The (4) four "jovian planets"; Jupiter, Saturn, Uranus, and Neptune have many moons each. Jupiter alone has 67 moons that we are aware of so far, while Saturn has more than 60 moons, Uranus has at least 27, and Neptune 14. There are at least (5) five additional so-called "dwarf planets" orbiting our sun beyond Neptune that we are aware of including Pluto, and there are at least (8) eight moons that we know of orbiting some of those "planets". Even the most accurately and beautifully descriptive words cannot appropriately appreciate the glorious complexities of God's creation (this universe).

When it comes to the modern lie about human evolution, scientists from different backgrounds of study have fallen prey to making observational correlations and then presuming causation. This is directly contrary to one of the most basic rules of science; "correlation is not causation". In other words, just because two different things are similar (people and monkeys for example), it can *never* be scientifically assumed that one of them has anything at all to do with the other one. The fact is, human beings did not evolve from chimpanzees nor anything else for that matter. In a **single human cell's** genes and chromosomes, there are as many individual bits of ***obviously intentionally organized*** information as there are letters in the world's largest public library; at the very least, 1 trillion…in only **one** cell. Individual letters in public libraries are obviously intentionally organized to produce different words in different books which produce completely different, but specific meanings in each book. *Each* word in *each* book is specifically intentional because each book conveys different and perfectly understandable information. In each book, the letters do not meaninglessly exist without purpose. Each letter in every single book in each library is organized to convey specific meanings, and any person who claims that books in public libraries spontaneously popped into existence, ***is still <u>less</u> confused*** than someone claiming that organic cells spontaneously formed. Most life forms on earth are comprised of multi-millions of cells, which are themselves perfectly organized to maintain and reproduce each species (See Chapter 6; *Genetics; A Way to Understand*). DNA (Deoxyribonucleic Acid) is designed (by God) so that the descendants of each species will continue to reproduce the same DNA, thereby producing the same species. Each species' DNA is specific to that species and does not change into other species, yet evolutionary scientists continue to claim (without any evidence at all) that human beings spontaneously evolved from some other animal after that animal had evolved from something else, and that one from something else, and so on and so forth. There are of course, *adaptational changes* that take place *within* species over periods of time but a swine is still a swine and a hippopotamus is still a hippopotamus, even though over time they may have become larger or smaller, more or less hairy, or have larger or smaller teeth, eyes, ears, etc. This is true for each and every species because God created them to be adaptable that way. Modern scientists' explanations and interpretations of fossilized bone fragments, animal teeth, skulls, etc., are commonly presented to the public as if evolution is a fact, but the only thing this so-called "evidence" has ever shown is that different kinds of people (Nephilim, people with dwarfism, people with big heads, little heads, tall people, short people, etc.) and pigs, bears, apes, chimpanzees, gorillas, and all sorts of other animals were alive at some point in the past. The term, "transitional species" refers to a life form which supposedly bridges a gap between two *different* species during an evolutionary change; a half-man, half-chimpanzee for instance. There are NO transitional species anywhere, and there never have been. Evolutionary lies permeate every aspect of modern science because people can naturally understand physical facts, but cannot naturally understand the spiritual truths about those facts outside of the knowledge of God in The Name of Jesus Christ. The Biblical account of human history is The Truth…period. Missing links are still missing ladies and gentlemen…. because they do not exist.

Modern scientists study physical matter in detail and the consistent production of replicable results produces a dangerous and misleading faith in physicality as a side effect. Physical consequences inevitably become predictable with repetition because every element in the physical realm was created by God to consistently maintain their given properties in spite of their physical states. Elements do not spontaneously change, they are always physically changed or combined for various reasons. They ARE what God created them to be and they consistently function accordingly. For example, two parts Hydrogen and one part Oxygen is still water whether it's vaporized, liquefied, frozen, or otherwise manipulated. The water is not going to spontaneously change into gasoline, lemon juice, or brake fluid. Also, because God created the elements to be stable, we can confidently make experimental predictions even after manipulating all kinds of different variables. We know for instance that at room temperature, oil will not mix with water very well and that sugar will; up to predictable saturation points. We can even change variables such as adding or reducing temperatures and sample amounts, and still confidently make accurate predictions with confidence because of this God-created stability. God knows what He is doing and He knew exactly what we were going to do. He **intended** for us to investigate His amazingly incredible creations, but here's the problem: **Interpretations of results** from scientific testing include making *assumptions and predictions*, and then forming new theories which go on to be tested. Those interpretations heavily influence what is financed for further research and to what extent. Most contemporary research interpretations (*assumptions, predictions, and new theories*) are evolutionarily biased, so explanations (consequential interpretations) of scientific study results are saturated with evolutionary dogma and untrue foolishness all stemming from a spiritually demonic desire to deny that God exists! Interpretations of experimental results are subject to spiritual influence and the author of confusion (the devil) negatively influences scientific interpretations using the primary excuse of the aforementioned separation of church and state. Separation of church and state to that degree is **indeed a good idea** for **any** society which **does** **not** acknowledge God in The Name of Jesus Christ because they are confused anyway, and **need** to separate "science" from "religion"; or "mythology" if you will. "Science" (any valid experimental investigation) when interpreted correctly, cannot be separated from the Truth because properly performed science ALWAYS validates that God created this universe and everything in it. Some of the major differences between "The Truth" and "religion (which includes atheism)" are discussed in the following chapter in detail.

There are many questions the big bang theory, the theory of evolution, and any other of the non-creation ideas cannot answer. Why haven't all of the lower animals evolved into human beings (or something even higher) after all this time since we are the top species and the spontaneous force behind evolution is each species' survival and proliferation? Where are the ones changing right now? How can similar looking, genetically different, *non-interbreeding* species exist if they evolved from each other? Atheists try and explain this away by saying that evolutionary changes occur in relatively short bursts of time and that this is why transitional species do not survive long and have not fossilized. This is yet another lie conjured up to try and explain why there is zero evidence that there has ever been a transitional species of any animal. Also, why would prey animals such as chickens, cows, mice, fish, wildebeests, rabbits, etc. (which human beings and other predators have always eaten) continue to exist without having spontaneously developed better defenses against consumption? *Answer*: Because God created them for us and other animals to eat; that's why! It is utterly ridiculous to think that certain animals spontaneously naturally select themselves to be prey for other species. Did the fictional force of evolution also decide that we needed those food sources and that we ourselves wouldn't be hunted, trapped, farmed out, cooked, eaten, captured for sport and placed into zoos, or held captive to be sold to other animals for food? No. Spontaneity makes no decisions at all, and it makes no sense to think that anything can be purposed, spontaneously. Spontaneity means the opposite of purpose and NOTHING in this physical realm is spontaneous, or has no purpose.....and we all know that everything has many purposes.

Early in the 1900's Anthropologists Charles Dawson and Martin A.C. Hinton intentionally filed down and changed the shapes of some fossilized bones they had found and said the bones represented the missing chimpanzee link to human evolution. They named the bones "Lucy", and the atheistic scientific community celebrated this "finding" as proof that God does not exist and that we had in fact spontaneously evolved. The hoax was later discovered and embarrassed the scientific community. The modern public atmosphere is primed for this kind of hoax to be accepted at face value again because of the modern eagerness to try and scientifically disprove God. The **worldwide public** today is indeed listening to false teachers. People everywhere have itching ears they want to be continually scratched with "new" information (2 Timothy 4:3KJV) and there are MANY examples of lies and hoaxes throughout the scientific community regarding the fictional big bang and the theory of evolution.

Societies worldwide respond in one way or another to scientific research in general, but scientifically researching things pertaining to the spirit realm is extremely difficult to perform with replicatable validity and in the next chapter, Chapter 4; "*MODERN SCIENCE: SPIRIT REALM RESEARCH*", I will explain why this is true.

CHAPTER FOUR

MODERN SCIENCE: SPIRIT REALM RESEARCH

Scientific research conducted to test for spiritual interactions in human circumstances requires different and higher test subject selection standards in order to produce valid results. For example, *deciding* whether or not **each** test subject in **each** spiritual study group is either "religious", or a truly "saved", born-again believer in the Biblical Word of God in The Name of Jesus Christ by His Holy Spirit, is a critical distinction to make because it directly determines the validity of those experiments. Study subjects (people) will be at different levels of "operational" spiritual belief/faith, or religion. A "*religious*" person for example, may go to church every Sunday and may adhere to most of the customs and traditions of "that particular group of people" with a believable kindness, but they may not have individual faith in Jesus Christ, The Son of God. They may not believe in their hearts that The God of the Holy Bible is the Comprehensive Source for ALL of their needs in The Name of Jesus Christ by His Holy Spirit; whereas on the other hand, a "***saved, born-again believer***" is a person who **knows** that God is all they need for everything in the Name of Jesus Christ by His Holy Spirit in **any** situation. They have faith. The problem with scientifically testing for spiritual interventions in human circumstances is, "How can the aforementioned test-subject distinctions be determined before every spiritual experiment to ensure validity?" That is a spiritual judgement. We *could* secretly film how potential test subjects handle challenging situations and circumstances in order to observe some spiritual and physical reactionary distinctions and then form experimental groups based on how they seem to have spiritually responded, but no; we will never be able to classify with any amount of scientific certainty, another person's relationship with God in Jesus' Name. We are not God, and we would certainly be attempting to sit in an **unattainable seat** of judgement if we took the approach of attempting to scientifically discern a person's salvation.

A person's behavior (religious or otherwise) is not necessarily indicative of what that person spiritually believes; therefore, it is difficult to make test subject distinctions which are reliable enough for spiritual experimental categorizations. As alluded to before, "**religion**" refers to *specific physical behaviors and activities seemingly carried out for spiritual purposes; good or evil, righteous or demonic*. Church customs and traditions, denominational activities, and many other such variables are all facets of religion, and individuals can be strictly "religious". "**Belief**" refers to *independent acknowledgement and belief in God in The Name of Jesus Christ, by His Holy Spirit*. A person's religious behaviors and activities can *sometimes* be an indicator of their level of belief, but this is a very unreliable way to try and determine someone's independent spiritual acknowledgement of God in The Name of Jesus Christ by His Holy Spirit. Again, this is critical to understand when attempting to research spiritual interactions and effects on human situations and circumstances. Faith in God in The Name of Jesus Christ *can indeed* change physical situations and circumstances, but the problem of being able to reliably separate *religious people* from *believers* **within** study groups for scientific experimentation has to be resolved in order to show this. This may be impossible to accomplish because like I said before, humans are not capable of making that particular spiritual determination reliably enough to produce valid experimental conclusions. The following; however, is very important to understand. Even if we **could** somehow reliably make the most accurate and valid spiritual test subject determinations for scientific experimental purposes, it still wouldn't matter. God's Holy Spirit is not subject to us and our sign-seeking verifications whether our desires are for scientific purposes or not (Mark 8:12; Luke 11:29; Matthew 16:4; KJV).

Because many influential scientists from all modern disciplines refuse to incorporate God into their understandings of physicality, then mainstream modern science is limited to studying and attempting to explain physical facts without the ability to understand the truth about those facts. Scientific study involves the manipulation of *physical variables* in order to learn more about them and the worldwide public is being duped by the devil via modern science into thinking that people have something to do with the existence of the physical variables we discover and study. This inevitably feeds atheistic mentalities when those same scientists explain physical variables as being nothing more than happenstance occurrences which they can explain without any mention of God having created them. This is unfortunately happening in **every** discipline of modern science because when scientists **discover** physical processes, systems, forces, or any other ongoing natural function in the universe (which were ALL engineered by God Almighty to work together), then why are those already existing functions and forces only credited to the people who discovered them with zero mention of The God that HAD TO HAVE created them? The functions are referred to as if they are the scientists' own **personal** "Laws" and "Principles". This goes on throughout modern science and like I said before, it only serves to water and fertilize already confused atheistic thought processes. Mankind **only discovers** processes, laws, and systems which God has already created and this is what **should be** continuously scientifically expressed, but as we all know; it is not. What does humanity have to do with already existing natural forces, functions, laws, mechanisms, wind patterns, ocean currents, tectonic plate movements, etc. We only discover them and either use or abuse them; that is all. For instance, "Kepler's Laws" mathematically describe already existing, perfectly organized relationships between the sun and the planets in our solar system. These perfectly balanced, **obviously designed** relationships have been ongoing since God created them, so how then can they be "Kepler's Laws"? Did Johannes Kepler place the planets where they are and did he do anything to keep the forces which keep them doing what they are doing in place? Of course NOT (Job 38:4 KJV). Another example is "Isaac Newton's Law of Universal Gravitation", which states that every particle in the universe attracts every other particle in the universe with varying degrees of force. Did Newton create that law, or did he only discover some aspects of gravity and write about it? Newton only discovered some aspects about gravity and documented them. Another example, "Blaise Pascal's Principle" states that changes in pressure applied to an enclosed fluid is transmitted undiminished to every point of the fluid, and to the walls of its container. Why is this referred to as "Pascal's Principle"? Did Pascal create this principle? No! He only figured out how to write a formula for understanding force parameters and other characteristics when it comes to contained fluids. Where was Pascal when God created force parameters?! "Archimedes' Principle", describes how and why objects float. Objects float because God created the buoyant forces and various conditions for floatation to take place. Again; Archimedes only described some of the mechanisms of displacement and buoyancy he realized were going on. This goes on and on along with a determined and intentional scientific emphasis on this existence being pointless and spontaneous.

Carbon is the only true "organic element" in existence because it is the only one existing in EVERY form of life there is, and mankind is THE ONLY PHYSICAL PURPOSE for the existence of any other physical life form. It is not a coincidence that The Bible calls the number 666 "the number of man" (Rev 13:18), and that Carbon atoms have 6 protons, 6 neutrons, and 6 electrons. This physical realm and every life form there is will pass away because it is ALL defiled with sin, so OF COURSE the name of the evil beast mentioned in The Bible is 666 (Rev 13:17).

Today's society is even confused about the obviously basic and natural differences between human males and females. When God created the **spirit** of man, He created us male and female (Gen 1:27; KJV). **After that**, He made a body from the earth He'd already created, and then blew the spirits of man (male and female) he'd already created in His image and likeness into that one physical body (Adam), "....and man became a living *soul*" (Gen 2:7 KJV). He **then** physically separated the female body from that same body (Gen 2:21-22; KJV), thereby separating the two *spiritually and physically different* human beings; a man and a woman (See "Creation", Page 5). The **very first thing** that happens when a man and a woman have sex and a baby is conceived (the instant the sperm penetrates the egg) is the physical determination of our sex; we are immediately either a physical boy or a girl (genetically/chromosomally). Cells immediately begin to multiply accordingly, and a baby then begins to grow inside the mother's womb. In very rare cases, *a physical body* develops with an unusual *physical* mixture of both male and female sexual organs caused by unusual physical combinations of the sex-determining X and Y chromosomes. Even in those situations, that person is spiritually either a male or a female and his/her physical sex-determining genetic chromosomes *physically manifest* that person as an obvious "majority" girl or "majority" boy. People are naturally spiritually, behaviorally, and physically obviously a man or a woman, but in modern societies worldwide, many people intentionally present themselves as androgynous and this only further confuses people's natural perceptions of sexuality. When people say, "I am a man/woman trapped in an opposite sex body", then they are inadvertently acknowledging (although with a confused twist) their *spiritual and physical* existence. Since *anything physical* can be naturally as well as intentionally manipulated, defiled, changed, etc., (human bodies during the physical birth process included), then there may be a tiny percentage of people whose natural sexual organs and physical bodies do not seem to reflect their spiritual beings. I am certainly not The Righteous Judge; so I don't know. Most modern claims as to males being trapped in female bodies and vice-versa however, are based on personal lifestyle preferences and desires as opposed to valid physical birth issues.

Only males have a "Y" chromosome, and sometimes they inherit extra "X" chromosomes (female chromosomes) during development (this is known as Klinefelter Syndrome). These males commonly possess higher voices, less body hair, a lower sperm count, or they may be asymptomatic altogether, but they are still "normal" males. Some males with this condition are sterile if they have a low sperm count, but this condition is not normally diagnosed until adulthood (20's and 30's) because it is not relevant until reproduction is attempted. Remember, ***anything physical*** can be manipulated and birth defects occur for various reasons and can occur at **any** place on the human body. Some people are born with defected arms, legs, heads, bodies, and sexual organs as well, but they are still whomever they are. The instant our sex is established (which is again, the very first thing which happens when a male's sperm fertilizes a female's egg), we become living souls; individual male or female spirits operating in individual physical realm bodies. I will discuss some spiritual and physical aspects of the human organism as it pertains to choices and behaviors in the next chapter; Chapter 5; *"THE PHYSICALITY OF REPROBATE PERCEPTIONS"*

CHAPTER FIVE

THE PHYSICALITY OF REPROBATE PERCEPTIONS

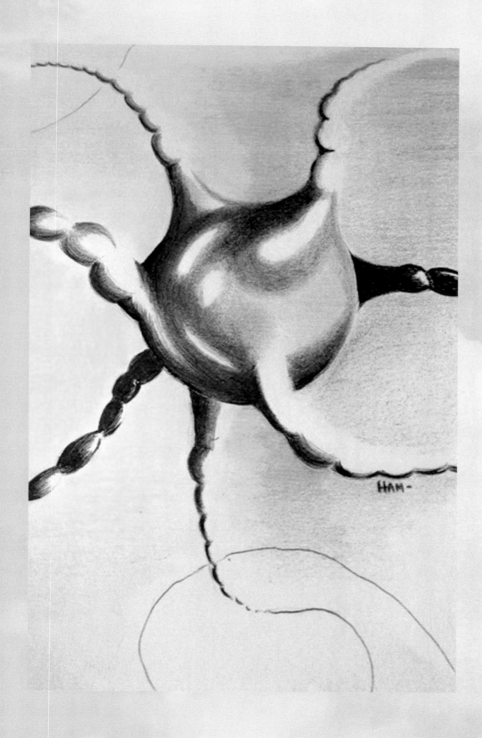

Why does it become more and more difficult for each of us to perceive good and evil in our own thoughts and behaviors after we've chosen to repeat those same thoughts and behaviors over an extended period of time? The answer is spiritual as well as physical because the actionable behaviors we express are physical manifestations of spiritual influences we decide to act on.

Remember, each human being is an individual spirit living inside a complex physical body (soul) which continuously converts righteous or demonic spiritual suggestions into intentional behaviors as decided on by each individual spirit. Each person's body however, has predispositional vulnerabilities due to its particular genetic makeup, and each body will physically influence the decisions each residing spirit (soul) ends up making due to biological (physical) parameters if you will. For instance, if a fella named Keith KNOWS that his granddaddy died at a young age due to cirrhosis of the liver caused by alcoholism, and that his daddy also died young from cirrhosis due to alcoholism, and that his mother is currently hospitalized because of the exact same issues, then Keith's decisions concerning how much alcohol he drinks will be influenced because he knows that most likely, alcohol will quickly negatively affect his liver. Keith can STILL choose to do whatever he wants to do concerning alcohol. He can use his free will to decide he will not drink alcohol at all under any circumstance, or Keith can drink alcohol every single day of his adult life if he chooses to do so. Biology *does not* determine behavior but it definitely *influences* the personal decisions we each make as independent thinkers. We make behavioral choices about everything we do in every situation and circumstance in spite of predisposed or any other influences, and we remember the **consequences** of those behavioral choices and subconsciously store those consequences in either long or short term memory depending on their importance to our physical survival and personal sentimental priorities. Memories of actual behaviors are not as influential on our future behaviors as are the **consequential memories** resulting from those same behaviors. Consequential memories are **memories of what happened as a result** of previous behaviors; *morals of the stories* if you will. The way each of us act around other people for instance, is mostly a culmination of consequential memories from the spiritually influenced behavioral actions we've previously undertaken around other people. We spiritually analyze the consequences of each and every behavior **we choose** to manifest to determine whether it was or whether it was not beneficial to us in any way, and to what extent. This is determined by our personal desires because we each have a free will and whether or not we deem our behaviors to be "good" or "evil" influences each individual differently. For example, if a married man is sexually interested in a woman he **knows** is married to someone else, yet he pursues her and begins a sexual relationship with her, he will naturally attempt to justify away his *feelings of guilt* relating to what he has done since she obviously was also sexually interested in him. Do his self-justifications have anything to do with changing what he has done? No they do not. We naturally attempt to justify our behaviors based on how we physically felt during situations and circumstances. Where do human beings' individual feelings of guilt before, during, and after we do evil come from? Human beings have natural feelings of guilt relating to unrighteous behaviors whether we attempt to ignore or repress those feelings or not, and just the FACT that feelings of guilt naturally coexist with negative human behaviors means that we are each unquestionably spiritually aware of "good" and "evil" (Genesis, Chapter 3 KJV).

Some people may think animals (especially dogs) are aware of good and evil but no; animals are not aware of good and evil. The fact that some animals *show obvious emotions* has nothing to do with them perceiving good and evil. For example, we can train **any kind of dog** to attack and kill small human babies and they will do it with no feelings of guilt. Whatever emotions those killer dogs ever express regarding attacking and killing human babies will **only** be geared towards their owners'/trainers' satisfaction level with them. The dogs' emotions will only be those of either excitement because they have satisfied their owners'/trainers' desires and the owners/trainers are happy because they have killed babies, or the dogs will display a sheepish disappointment because they know that they did not kill any babies and therefore will not be rewarded. Animals do not perceive good and evil; only human beings do and no, we are not animals!

The adulterous man in the earlier example manifested the entire idea of having sex with a married woman from a negative spiritual influence (a demon), and after his first sexual affair with her, he most likely had very strong feelings of guilt as one of his consequential memories. He will remember things about her depending on the amount of physical pleasure or displeasure he'd experienced with her because resulting guilty feelings become progressively less associated with consequential memories from repeated behaviors when those repeated behaviors continually produce positive or pleasurable feelings. The opposite is also true as well because guilty feelings become more associated with consequential memories from repeated behaviors when those repeated behaviors produce negative feelings, except in people who are sociopathic or otherwise insensitive (reprobate; which I will clarify later in this chapter).

"Adultery man's" future behavioral manifestations regarding this married woman will still depend on which spiritual influences he contemporarily chooses to listen to (either Holy or evil), but those choices will be heavily influenced by already existing consequential memories from his previous sexual encounters with her. Perhaps the affair was problematic, stressful, and negative for him because not only did they get caught by her husband, but he contracted a sexually transmitted disease from the married woman, and she's now also pregnant with what may be his child. Those are very negative consequences and his feelings of guilt will be stronger and last longer than they otherwise would have. If, on the other hand he had a very pleasurable sexual experience with her and they both had a great time, didn't get caught, no venereal diseases were contracted, and she is not pregnant, then his strong feelings of guilt will probably not last as long. Whatever the results turn out to be, the *consequences* of what happened will undoubtedly affect his behavior towards her from then on and will most likely generalize to his sexual thoughts and behaviors towards other married women in the future. This is an example of how *consequential memories* can affect future behaviors. Again, memories of actual behaviors are not as influential on future behaviors as are the consequential memories gleaned from those behaviors. Of course the man in this adultery example will remember some of the actual physical positions and feelings which occurred during their sexual interludes, but his consequential memories will more heavily influence his future decisions. Our choices regarding which spiritual influences we listen to (Holy or demonic), our ultimate physical actions, and our individual abilities to righteously spiritually analyze our own behavioral consequences are directly related to salvation in Jesus' Name (or the lack thereof). Our personal long and short-term goals and desires, as well as our individual determinations to do what we want to do, all strongly influence how we utilize consequential memories. We spiritually classify the consequences of our chosen behaviors according to self-perceived, self-preservational needs, and the information from personally desirable behavioral consequences is consciously used as much as possible by each of us in different situations. This repetitious usage of the same consequential information in different situations and circumstances becomes recognizable as a behavioral consistency, and we call behavioral consistencies, personalities.

Sometimes our brain neurons are basically forced to associate previously unassociated consequential memories with new consequential memories. As we consistently choose to manifest particular behaviors (personality development), we become more and more experienced in those choices and we begin to relate more and more previously unassociated consequential information with each behavioral choice. The more that neurons in the brain progressively include previously unassociated consequential information, the more convinced we become that our current behaviors are justified. The dendrites of our brain neurons extend out like tree roots and make different consequential contacts as we solidify behaviors. This makes it progressively harder and harder for us to change our behaviors regardless of whether they are "good" or "evil". If a person likes being by himself/herself for example, and they know that if they act certain ways or say certain things that people will leave them alone because they think they are mean, then they are only thinking that way because they have consequential memories from previous interactions with people using similar techniques and words that made people leave them alone. These same mental processes are also at work for example, when linebackers playing American football hit opposing running backs extra hard on plays when the running backs do not have the ball. If the consequences normally result in less than average games for those running backs, then the linebackers will continue to do that and their teams gain defensive advantages. The linebackers may not remember each hit in each game, but they remember the consequences of executing those hits. An interesting point is that positive consequential memories about particular activities, combined with the physical ability to perform those activities very well, increases one's ability to produce their desired positive results. This is especially true when it comes to competitive sports, and when physically gifted people recognize this fact at a young age, we get great athletes like Michael Jordan, Tom Brady, Cynthia Cooper, Muhammed Ali, LeBron James, Florence Griffith Joyner, Tiger Woods, Roger Clemons, Sue Bird, Edson Arantes do Nascimento, (Pele'), and the absolute litany of other fantastically gifted athletes like Jackie Joyner Kersey and Walter Payton for instance.

Consequential perceptions are *physically* represented in the brain via synapse connections between various memory storage neurons and can therefore be changed or rewired so to speak. Stereotypical thoughts for example, are not always formed by choice, nor are they necessarily correctly spiritually self-perceived as being "good" or "evil". For example, was it "right" or "wrong" for an African-American man who was born and raised in a segregated southern American town during the early 1900s to think that *all* white people were mean, evil, negative, and violent if all of the white people he had experienced in his lifetime had been mean, evil, negative and violent towards black people? Were his negative thoughts about white people justified? With each incident of racial hatred he either heard about or personally experienced, his consequential perceptions from those memories stimulated and further strengthened the physical synapse connections already established in his brain which stored negative consequential memories regarding white people. Nevertheless, as *we all* mature from children into adults, we become more and more spiritually responsible for evaluating ourselves for righteousness in every aspect. We must each spiritually examine our existing thought patterns, stereotypes, and our manifested general behaviors. In our physical brains, the already routed synapse connections making various memory associations (consequential memories) are what we individually filter our contemporary spiritual influences and ultimately expressed behaviors through. This is how a person can spiritually KNOW they are wrong about having negative thoughts or beliefs about other kinds of people for instance, yet continue to manifest negative behaviors towards those same people. If already existing, physically formed thought patterns (brain neuron synaptic connections) and consequential memory associations are not spiritually self-investigated for righteousness and corrected (rewired) with The Truth, then brain synapse connections will continue to strengthen as they are and make it progressively more and more difficult for us to change negative thoughts and expressed behaviors towards other people. This is clearly indicated when people say things like, "That's just the way those people are!", or "I've always known that about those people anyway!", while trying to justify saying or doing something negative to them. Some people attempt to justify murdering men, women, and children because of their different races, religious beliefs, lifestyles, etc.

God will give us over to a reprobate mind if we decide to keep choosing negative behaviors (Romans 1:28-32 KJV) and that means a person will not receive any more righteous spiritual suggestions. Without righteous suggestions (from the Holy Spirit), it is difficult to express behaviors which go against negative synaptic "hardwiring" in the brain. A reprobate person has lost the spiritual ability to consider the negative consequences of particular behaviors because the physical brain neuron connections which manifest negative behaviors when spiritually stimulated have been used too many times in too many different situations. They are also less able to recognize how their abnormal behaviors or actions are perceived by other people. For example, a reprobate person on drugs (because at an earlier time in their lives *they decided* they would not stop using despite numerous warnings and opportunities to stop) shows little concern for how they are acting around other people in their immediate area, even though they may be standing on top of a car at 3a.m. loudly singing Christmas carols …. in July. When people do things like this they are immediately perceived by other "normal" people as being potentially dangerous because they are acting outside of the bounds of normal public behavior. People who have callously murdered people before and will readily kill again with no remorse, and people who are habitual liars for instance, are reprobate people concerning those behavioral sins. Remember, behaviors are physical manifestations of spiritual suggestions we decide to act on, so when we choose to keep doing particularly negative and unGodly behaviors, then we become vulnerable to being given over (by God) to a reprobate mind regarding those particular behaviors. When this happens, God will no longer communicate righteous suggestions to us concerning what we're doing, and we are then left to the woes of manifesting behaviors from stored negative consequential memories regarding those particular areas of conduct.

"Being evil", and "doing evil things" are two different things. For example, if a man has had sexual experiences with other men during a particularly curious phase of his life and he later ceased those behaviors, then he is not "gay". That man committed those sins, but he did not continue in them to the point of reprobation and he is not claiming to be gay. A self-confessed "gay" man is indeed reprobate concerning homosexuality. If a person has told lies before (and we all have), then he/she is not necessarily reprobate concerning lying, unless they are a "habitual liar". A habitual liar is a person who continuously tell lies (even about petty things) for no reason. They are reprobate concerning lying. Because someone has stolen something before, that does not make them a kleptomaniac (a habitual thief who is reprobate concerning stealing), but a person who takes pride in stealing and does so on a regular basis is indeed reprobate concerning thievery.

When we are born, our souls, personalities, and basic temperaments are the same as they will always be. We are who we are and we each experience different and independent existences which influence our individual perceptions as we develop. We are born into this world in a small, physically uncoordinated, unprogrammed "machine" (body), and we each perceive the world through our own bodies as we grow and learn. We continually develop abilities to communicate better and better so we can share each other's perceptions of life in many different ways unlike anything else in physical existence. We are spirits existing in bodies which are slowly and continuously changing in various ways as they grow larger and stronger and more capable as physically "governed" by genetics. As we spiritually exist in these physical bodies, we are each aware of how we are being perceived by others and if we are not, then there is a problem. Parents and other responsible adults in societies worldwide teach children culturally relevant behavioral norms and parameters, and each "normal" person in a civil society is consistently aware of his or her public behaviors. This helps us define ranges of how we behave around others such as how we construct our sentences, how we walk, smell, talk, dress, etc., and normally people do not want to be perceived as being dangerous, psychotic, or abnormal based on how they operate in public.

We each need to investigate ourselves when it comes to maintaining negatively formed thoughts and behaviors towards other people no matter how seemingly justifiably they were formed. Some people decide not to change at all and go through their lives full of hatred and confusion. The African American man who grew up in the segregated south for example, is still **not** justified if he goes through the rest of his life hating or negatively stereotyping *all* white people because of his personal experiences. Although it is certainly understandable for him to have negative consequential memories about white people which may manifest as negative thoughts and behaviors towards the entire race, he is still spiritually responsible as an adult to check his mindsets and behaviors for righteousness so as *not to* errantly generalize his negative stereotypical thinking to all white people. The sooner he does this, the less likely he is to become reprobate concerning his negative thoughts and perceptions because of the previously discussed reasons. The white people who caused his negative thoughts and perceptions to occur in the first place were most likely already reprobate concerning hating black people. They had inevitably become *physically* bound to translating negative spiritual influences into negative behaviors against black people (they were reprobate). We are ALL born into this sinful physical realm and we ALL need to be "mentally rewired" in order to attain righteous thinking. *Righteous rewiring* occurs **only** through salvation in the Name of Jesus Christ by the renewing of the mind by the Holy Spirit of God (Romans 12:2; Ephesians 4:23; KJV). Our behaviors are conscious, personal decisions we make on a continual basis and reprobate or not, we will each ultimately be held accountable for our manifested behaviors.

In Chapter 6, *"GENETICS; A WAY TO UNDERSTAND"*, I will discuss some interesting ways to understand the genetics of these human bodies we have been placed in. Chapter 6 should also help you better understand genetic research in general and why we humans are **each** indeed special, uniquely created beings.

(CHAPTER SIX)

GENETICS; A WAY TO UNDERSTAND

Writing is an ability we use to intentionally communicate with each other using *precisely arranged letters* to convey specifically detailed meanings. Mankind's God-given ability to linguistically communicate (read and write) provides opportunities for us to be able to better appreciate some of the complexities of organic genetics. Biological expressions of seemingly insignificant, individual nucleotides in human DNA; Adenine (A), Cytosine (C), Guanine (G), and Thiamine (T), can be directly compared to expressions of individual letters in any alphabet and in any language which make up words and sentences when human beings communicate. In each different language there are deeper expressions of letters and letter combinations such as long sounds, short sounds, silent letters, blended letters, etc. Although there are only 26 letters available to us in the English language, this still allows us to make a myriad of specific words which each manifest precise, independent meanings.

"Words" are intentional initiations of spiritual to physical manifestations because they are physical vehicles for spiritual transportation/transference. For example, if a husband wrote something on a piece of paper and gave it to his wife as they sat together somewhere, she would probably take the paper and start reading it. If, after reading what was written, she becomes physically enraged and obviously emotionally hurt and leaves the area crying, then he was able to give her something physical which emotionally affected her (emotions are physically expressed, spiritual moods). Words alone caused her reaction. The woman reacted as she did because the piece of paper her husband gave her read, "I really did have sex with your mother last night and I think I am in love with her."

Words indeed transport spirits and *each letter* in each word has potentials to be powerfully influential in many ways. There can be major differences in the overall expressions of books for instance, if only a few letters in only a few of the words are different in specific places. For instance, if one book has "could" and another of the exact same title has "couldn't" in only one pivotal place, or "his" instead of "hers", or "died" instead of "did", etc., then the overall expressions of each of those books would be significantly altered in various ways and the same thing is true in genetics. In DNA, each nucleotide can be powerfully influential to the manifestation of any of the parts of a physical organism in the same way, including causing birth defects. Nucleotide positional differences cause different physical manifestations in each member of each species making them each different from each other; differently individual puppies from the same litter for instance.

"Martin did like everyone else." for example, is significantly different from a sentence stating, "Martin died like everyone else." There is only a *one* letter difference between the two sentences, but the first sentence means that a lot of people were doing something and Martin did the same thing everybody else was doing, while the second sentence communicates an entirely different meaning which stimulates entirely different emotions. It means that everybody is dead including Martin. If these sentences were the last sentences in two different but otherwise similar books about "Martin", then these two books would express completely different overall meanings. Remember; that powerful difference was caused by only one letter and although the books' titles are the same and they look the same, the books are different….as is each member of each species. The books however, are still not going to spontaneously turn into magazines, videos, DVDs, nor anything else, any more than monkeys spontaneously turned into humans.

The same "letter" may occur often throughout a written story **or** throughout the genetic codes of organisms' DNA chains, and each "letter's" influence can range from being functionally insignificant, to being absolutely critical depending on its location. None of this has anything to do with one species being able to spontaneously change into another species. We scientifically know that this is impossible, just as a book spontaneously changing into a video or anything else would be impossible. God specifically designed each life form.

The nucleotides Adenine (A), Cytosine (C), Guanine (G), and Thiamine (T), obviously possess multi-variable qualities comparable to alphabetic letters, but right now we do not understand how and when most of those qualities are expressed. We will probably never *fully* understand those qualities either, so because we have the *ability* to physically manipulate genes, chromosomes, nucleotides, etc., *that doesn't mean that we should do so* in reckless, and inconsiderate manners. Genetic research on animals produces many results that "don't make sense" right now because we're misplacing "letters" and "misspelling" so many words. Overall "meanings" are confused and physical results are irrevocably deformed and strangely different, such as creatures with misplaced eyes, too many legs, deformed body parts, etc. **There is nothing wrong with conducting science** (1 Timothy 6:20-21) and God intended for us to investigate and marvel at His glorious creations, as long as we understand and acknowledge that they are indeed, "His creations".

"Science" is the professional way we learn about and document this physical realm but when the **motivation** for conducting science is trying to disprove the Biblical account of creation, then "science" will inevitably lead to blasphemous confusion every single time. Genetic studies show that our bodies are incredible machines designed with the same biological concepts and mechanisms as a lot of other organic creations in this physical existence, and sometimes there are only small genetic differences between different species. Human beings are almost genetically identical to mice, pigs, chimpanzees, and many other creatures, but this in no way means that we evolved from any other animal after going through some sort of lucky, spontaneous biological changes. That is as ridiculous as houseflies "knowing" that the box of cereal on my refrigerator spontaneously evolved from a smaller cardboard box in my garage because they look similar and are constructed with some of the same materials. The boxes may have even been designed by the same person in the same factory using the same materials, but each box has its own purpose and each box was indeed intelligently and independently designed and constructed for those purposes.

Because of the complexities within the genetic realm alone, it is not at all possible that we are happenstance beings. Our bodies are complex physical machines which God individually designed to translate spiritual suggestions (Holy or demonic) into desired physical actions as per the will of the spiritual host; you (See Chapter 4; "*Attentional Awareness*"). I absolutely LOVE that explanation. God created all kinds of different life forms and *He designed* specific nucleotide positional arrangements for each member of each species. Particular genetic arrangements within each species produce specific physical characteristics such as hair color, height and weight potentials, skin color, teeth arrangements, kneecap designs, metabolisms, and everything else physical. God created innumerable physically inter-related, consequence producing systems of all kinds everywhere, and these physical systems can all be manipulated and used for good or evil purposes. Just because God created the same "genetic letters" and arranged them differently for each particular form of life, then some modern scientists assume a spontaneous, evolutionary process took place.

If I were to write a short comedy skit for a high school play, and then write a long tragic novel for publication, how would these writings relate to each other? Would one story have spontaneously written itself after physically evolving from the other one? Of course not, and we all know that this would be a ridiculous impossibility. Even if I used the same pen to write some of the same words to describe some similar situations in each of the writings, the words could not change themselves to be anything different from what I originally intended for them to be. Both writings would be letters grouped together to make up words I've intentionally arranged to express my intended meanings and no; the writings have nothing to do with the existence of each other except for the fact that they were written by the same author. Amen.

Human beings know chimpanzees are not humans and there is no natural confusion about that in either species. When chimpanzees see us, they naturally recognize that we are not chimpanzees at all. Scientists who say that human beings evolved from chimpanzees continue to emphasize the point that there is only about a three percent genetic difference between humans and chimps, but what does that mean? Don't be mislead; the "three percent" genetic difference in the nucleotides in the functioning genes between humans and chimpanzees literally represents *millions of <u>obvious</u>* external and internal differences between the two organisms. If I wrote two similar, 11,000 page books with 320 pages worth of completely different letters including the covers and titles (between humans and chimpanzees, 320 book pages represents about a 3% genetic difference between our "books"), then the manifested differences could range all over the place. If those "320 pages worth of different letters (words)" were in critical places and expressed extreme differences between the books (such as "did" and "died"), then those books may still look similar, but the obvious differences would be plainly manifested just as they are between human beings and chimpanzees, pigs, goats, dogs, and any other animal we are genetically similar to. Remember; the "did" and "died" example was only one letter's worth of difference, so imagine what can happen with 320 pages worth of letter (words) differences in any book.

Again, there are **trillions** of nucleotides in human DNA, and they can each manifest or influence different aspects of physical characteristics. Some of these characteristics are visually obvious and some are less physically obvious, but regardless; the manifested differences between individual human beings as well as any other animal and their characteristics are blatantly obvious. There was no spontaneous beginning, and there is no such thing as evolution as far as one species spontaneously changing into another via natural selection or any other proposed method.

Each human being was independently created by God; The Omnipotent, Omnipresent, Almighty Creator, for His purposes and He gave each of us a free spiritual will so we can do and believe as we please while still being cognizant of good and evil. It literally takes a place as large as this universe to contain us. God knows what He is doing. There was no spontaneous beginning, and we did NOT EVOLVE from anything! May God eternally bless each of you to acknowledge and believe in His Pure Righteousness and Word in The Name of Jesus Christ by His Holy Spirit! We are indeed mankind; God's most awesome creation. Jesus Christ; Almighty God in the flesh, told us the world would NOT believe The Truth, and so it is. Remember; The Truth NEVER changes because someone decides they do not want to believe it, so *do not choose* to be a non-believer. The negative consequences of eternal damnation are far too great. God only asks that we believe He came here in a human body (Jesus), and that He physically became all sin and killed it (when He physically died) and left it dead when He resurrected. Jesus is soon to spiritually return for those of us who believe, and we need to have the same level of faith, trust, and confidence in Jesus that small children naturally have in their parents. Jesus Christ is NOT the little hippie-looking guy in those pictures which have been circulated all over the world either. That is a demonic lie. Jesus was not a physically "handsome" man. He was in fact the opposite, and so much so that He was difficult to look at; this makes perfect sense (Isaiah Chapter 53).

We do not know God's original purposes as far as the "why's" about *ANYTHING*. Physical existences are intimately complex and mean a lot more than any of us have the ability to understand right now. No; you are NOT just some happenstance left over star dust as the devil and most of his **modern** scientists would have you to believe! May God bless you in Jesus' Name.

I've told you the Truth; I pray you learned something that will bless your life.

MANKIND; GOD'S MOST AWESOME CREATION

(The True Origin of Man)

Human Beings: The *human* spirit (the spirit of man) in different physical human bodies, *being* individual souls.

FACT: God created the *human spirit* male and female in His image (Genesis 1:27 KJV), and *then* God put that spirit into each male or female body to exist as individual souls (Genesis 2:7KJV).

FACT: The Word of God separates the three components of man (spirit, body, soul) and discerns us there....at our deepest. (Hebrews 4:12KJV)

FACT: We each have a free will and we can each do whatever we want to do, but there are ultimate consequences for our thoughts and behaviors, both good and evil.